## Some other works by Peter FitzSimons

*Basking in Beirut and Other Adventures*
*Nick Farr-Jones*
*Hitch-hiking for Ugly People*
*The Rugby War*
*Everyone but Phar Lap*
*FitzSimons on Rugby*
*Beazley*
*Nancy Wake*
*John Eales*
*Nene*
*Steve Waugh*
*Great Australian Sports Champions*
*Little Theories of Life*
*The Ballad of Les Darcy*
*Tobruk*
*Kokoda*
*Charles Kingsford Smith and Those Magnificent Men*
*A Simpler Time*
*Mawson*
*Batavia*
*Eureka*
*Ned Kelly*
*Gotta Love This Country!*
*Seriously . . . you have to laugh*
*Victory at Villers-Bretonneux*
*Burke & Wills*
*Gallipoli*
*Fromelles and Pozières*
*Mutiny on the Bounty*

# PETER FITZSIMONS

## FAIR GO, SPORT

### INSPIRING AND UPLIFTING TALES OF GOOD FOLKS, GREAT SPORTSMANSHIP AND FAIR PLAY

ALLEN&UNWIN

SYDNEY•MELBOURNE•AUCKLAND•LONDON

Cover images: John Eales, Dallas Kilponen/Fairfax Syndication;
Betty Cuthbert, Fairfax Syndication; Michelle Payne on Prince of Penzance,
Joe Arma/Fairfax Syndication; Norm Provan and Arthur Summons,
John O'Gready/Fairfax Syndication.

First published in 2018
This edition published in 2019

Allen & Unwin
83 Alexander Street
Crows Nest NSW 2065
Australia
Phone:   (61 2) 8425 0100
Email:   info@allenandunwin.com
Web:    www.allenandunwin.com

A catalogue record for this
book is available from the
National Library of Australia

ISBN 978 1 76087 692 0

Set in Minion by Midland Typesetters, Australia
Printed and bound in Australia by SOS Print + Media Group

10 9 8 7 6 5 4 3 2

# Contents

# Contents

# Introduction

The idea for this book is simple. In the year when Australian cricketers have colluded to nakedly cheat, when attendance rates for all of soccer, rugby union and rugby league have either drifted or roared south, there is an obvious disaffection with modern sport and all the grubbiness that has come with it.

Over the last thirty odd years, in articles and books, I have tried, among other things, to capture the best, most inspiring, and most heart-warming tales of sports, together with profiling the characters who gave us that magic—or at the very least, *engaged* us. One thing that became apparent over the years was that there was frequently more reaction to stories about unknowns and golden greats of yesteryear than the modern big bird professionals.

What follows is a collection of what I regard as the best of such tales. Most, but not all, are Australian based. Ideally, they represent the best of sport, or at least the most alluring and inspirational, before the 'serious-ification' of the whole shebang started to squeeze the life out of it on so many different levels at once.

I do hope you enjoy the reading as much I enjoyed the writing and gathering.

Peter FitzSimons
June 2018
Sydney

# THE INSPIRATIONAL

*'Every morning in Africa a gazelle wakes up. It knows it must move faster than the lion or it will not survive. Every morning a lion wakes up and it knows it must move faster than the slowest gazelle or it will starve. It doesn't matter if you are the lion or the gazelle, when the sun comes up, you better be moving.'*
The late, great Roger Bannister on life.

*'We'll still love you whether you kick it or not.'*
Wallabies' captain David Pocock as he handed the ball to stand-in kicker Mike Harris to kick a goal to win or lose the Test against Wales in Melbourne 2012. It was only Harris' second Test. He kicked it.

*'I thought competing in the yellow suit was tough, but Sally [Pearson] is out there doing it in her bra and undies!'*
Anna Meares with the quote of the 2016 Rio Games.

# A classic tale

In March of 1956, down Melbourne way, they held Olympic trials and in the 1500m young Ron Clarke, a teenager, found himself up against a star-studded field that included the best distance runner in the country, John Landy.

From the gun the runners went out hard.

Clarke was up near the front of the field, while race-favourite Landy sat in behind, planning for a strong finish.

Turning the bend with 600m to go, the flying feet of one of the runners extended the barest fraction too much and clipped the heels of young Ron.

'I was down on the track before I even knew what happened,' Clarke once told me.

For Landy, just behind him and closing fast when it happened, it was like the way it is when you've hit the brakes on a wet road and are sliding forward, powerless to stop, whatever you do. For as Clarke sprawled on the track before him, Landy was unable to avoid bringing his right foot down, and his spikes went into Clarke's left shoulder.

Still, Landy had kept his balance and was entirely capable of running on.

But he didn't. He was concerned Clarke had been really hurt, so he stopped and turned back to help him up.

'Are you all right, Ron?' he asked.

'Yes! Yes! Go! Go! Run!' Clarke replied.

When Landy continued on in the race, the rest of the field had by this time moved 35m ahead . . . and the rest could have been taken straight from a Boy's Own book on running heroes.

With the crowd screaming themselves hoarse, willing him faster so as to catch the other runners, Landy tore after them, covering the next 200m from that point in an almost unbelievable 25 seconds and, of course, he went on to win.

# Super story that

The legendary English journalist Ian Wooldridge of *Daily Mail* fame was one day playing golf with his great friend Richie Benaud and faced a shocker of an approach shot over an expanse of water. Fearing what was going to happen, Wooldridge replaced his new ball with a somewhat bruised and cracked older one from the depths of his bag. Benaud, ever the sportsman, noted his rival's caution and, reaching into his own bag, tossed Wooldridge a virgin ball still in its cellophane wrapper.

'Use that,' he instructed. Though he didn't say it, his point was clear. By reaching for the older ball, Wooldridge was conceding the shot would go awry before even hitting it and . . .

And I am sure you are way ahead of me. For, of course, Wooldridge stepped up and smacked the ball beautifully, to see it land within trickling distance of the hole. He looked across at his opponent.

Benaud gave him a lovely wry smile. Ever the master of the significant pause, he knew that nothing needed to be said.

In the words of reader Allastair McGilvray, who sent me the story, 'Bless you Richie. When you were at the mic it was always summer.'

# Two great golden girls

It was one of the great moments in Australian sport. You see, when Raelene Boyle won gold in her last race, at the Brisbane Commonwealth Games in 1982—roaring home in the 400 metres—the stadium roared even as the nation came to a standstill. Raelene, a beloved figure, who had been denied gold in the previous two Olympics at the hands of East Germans (say no more), had at least and at last the perfect finish to her career. And who has been organised to present the medal at such an emotion-charged, proud, national moment? Why, none other than Betty Cuthbert!

Betty, a legend of her own time, had three Olympic gold medals to her credit from a quarter-century earlier, before she contracted multiple sclerosis—which is why in 1982 she was mostly wheelchair-bound. But not for this occasion!

No, to give Raelene her medal, Betty is determined to do it on her own two feet, and now, painfully, slowly, makes her way forward unaided right to the dais in the centre of the stadium. As the crowd roars even more, she presents the bronze and silver medals, and now reaches up with the gold medal to put it around the neck of the crowd's heroine, while the big screen flashes the very words the announcer is intoning to the stadium, 'RAELENE—OUR GOLDEN GIRL.'

But now, as Raelene leans further forward, it brings her mouth in proximity to Betty's ear, enabling her to whisper, 'Don't believe it. There's only one golden girl. And it's you, Betty Cuthbert.'

Betty's knees buckle with emotion. And yet, though hands reach out to support her, she waves them away, stands tall for the national anthem, then makes her way, still upright and unaided, 100 metres or more back into the bowels of the stadium—using all those qualities of pride, resilience and strength that had made her such a champion all those years ago.

Just one step inside the tunnel, however, the instant she is out of public view, she collapses into the arms of officials. There is a flood of tears, of pain from the multiple sclerosis and sheer emotion. It takes a while, but after she sobs out the story of what Raelene had said to her on the dais, everyone within earshot is crying too.

Nigh on two decades later, at the Sydney Olympics, tens of thousands of spectators cheered Betty on as she entered the stadium—pushed in her wheelchair by none other than Raelene—carrying the Olympic torch.

Betty died in August 2017, aged 79 in Mandurah, Western Australia.

# A fitting farewell

There were many high points to the state funeral of former Wallaby captain and key ARU president, Sir Nicholas Shehadie, at St James Church on Wednesday, but none higher than the wonderful eulogy delivered by his son, Michael, starting with the account of the birth of his father, when the doctor said to his mother, 'Congratulations, Mrs Shehadie, you've just delivered a baby elephant.' It brought the house down—a house that included *le tout* Sydney, starting with three former prime ministers, the Governor-General and the Premier, and continuing with the likes of Bob Dwyer, Simon Poidevin and Nick Farr-Jones.

One of Michael's themes was the humble beginnings of Sir Nicholas in the mean streets of Redfern, and how he never lost that humility, or the strong friendships he formed there.

'He fondly remembered those days with his friends,' Michael said, 'and once told me that whilst he was Lord Mayor there wasn't one garbage strike in the city, as all the garbos had grown up with him.'

Sir Nicholas' wife of 61 years, Dame Marie Bashir, sat in the front row, in elegant black, and laughed lightly, and knowingly.

When it came to the story of their romance, however, Michael outdid himself.

With great pride, Michael recounted how it started in 1953, when he was a famous, hulking Wallaby prop and she was a petite medical student at Sydney University.

'The relationship was a surprise to many who regarded their interests as very different,' Michael recounted. 'But it was a simple gesture that won my mother's heart. Mum was undertaking a student paediatrics term at the Royal Alexandra Hospital for Children. She was caring for a desperately ill child who had recently been abandoned by his family. There were no visitors or toys. Naturally, Mum was deeply distressed and told Nick of her sadness for the child. The next day, Mum walked into the hospital to find the little boy's cot filled with toys and teddy bears.'

Again, it brought the house down. That was the Sir Nicholas we knew and loved.

At funeral's end as the coffin was placed in the hearse, and the crowd pressed close, the clear sound of a referee's whistle pealed, playing that distinctive tune. Full-time, Sir Nicholas. Well played. And too many victories to count.

# No stoppin' Kurt

In late 2006 I received an email from a young bloke who said he'd like to chat, face-to-face, about doing the Kokoda Track. As I had done a book about it, and had walked it, he thought I could give him some tips.

Sure.

We arranged to meet for breakfast the following week at a café. He turned up right on time and I was . . . surprised.

For the fellow that turned up was in a wheelchair.

'Is it feasible,' he asked, 'for me to crawl the Kokoda Track?'

That was an easy one.

No. It was a physical torture that gutted the able-bodied, let alone those with a disability. So, despite your courage in even thinking about it, the answer is no, *no*, NO.

Still, he was a lovely bloke, about 25 years old, and he told me something of his story. Born in that lost speck of a town called Carcoar, in western NSW, with a condition that affected the lower part of his spine, he had never been able to walk, and he'd made the best of things thereafter. What helped enormously was being the youngest of a large and loving family, all of whom told him he could bloody well do anything he wanted, regardless. And Carcoar felt the same. He was 14 when some of the fine citizens of that town decided to put money together to get him a wheelchair racer, and send him to Denver to race.

'My parents tried to stop them,' Kurt recounted, 'but they said, 'You stay out of this—it's between us and the young fella.'

In two weeks they'd raised ten grand, and he was soon on his way, winning the race for his age division.

'My whole world changed,' he said. 'I realised there were people just like me, and lots of them. I'd found my community. They changed my life.'

Fabulous!

But, crawl Kokoda?

I repeat: No.

Of course this young man—Kurt Fearnley, seeing as you ask—ignored my advice, and did indeed crawl the whole way. He dedicated his feat to Corporal Tony Metson who, back in 1942, had taken a bullet to the ankle at the Battle of Isurava, and who subsequently crawled the whole way back, refusing to be borne on a stretcher—he reckoned they were for the blokes who were worse off than him.

16

# Michelle, our belle

Most of us felt that, when it comes to horse racing, stories just don't get any better than Phar Lap—the once-in-a-century horse that won the Melbourne Cup in 1930, carrying the hopes of a nation and no few mortgages on his back. But then we were forced to take a really close look at the events that unfolded on the first Tuesday of November in the year 2015. This was the stuff of life, the stuff of sport: ups and downs, swings and roundabouts, yin and yang . . . this was the Ballad of Prince of Penzance!

For if there is one thing that rivals this nation's delight in a champion proving itself to be just that, it is an underdog that proves to be a champion after all. And when you have an underdog riding an underdog, and the top underdog proves to have a back-story that would kill a brown dog, well, friends, you are in story heaven. For this yarn, start with the horsey, Prince of Penzance. A no-hoper. Dog-food in a still ambulant pose. Never got close to winning a major race. Constantly broke down. History of sickness and injury. Getting old now. Six years old! When its odds came in at 101-1, some experts were surprised that the odds weren't higher.

'Couldn't win the race with a 100m head start and a jetpack on their rear fetlocks,' one form guide described the six-year-old. 'Prince of Penzance has a good trainer, jockey and barrier. But if you draw him in your office sweep, your best bet is to swap tickets sneakily with the office drunk. Either that or quit your job.' Even the owners—six mates, composed of a 'butcher, baker, candlestick maker, rich man, poor man, beggar man'—had little faith.

For such a horse, getting a top-line jockey was out of the question. All they could manage was to get a jockey who, up until a decade or two ago, was the most unheard of thing anyone had ever heard of in racing—a *sheila* competing against men. She'd won five Group 1 races but was not given much hope in the Cup. And, of course, no woman had ever won the mighty Melbourne Cup.

Besides, outside the racing community, Michelle Payne was more anonymous than a wrong number. And she even came close to quitting when, first of all, she was nearly killed by a fall in 2004, and then she took a bad tumble that near broke her back a couple of years ago. But she persisted, through both. But, of course, the wonder of her story didn't stop there. She had had to overcome many obstacles to get there, including being the youngest of ten who'd lost her mother when she was just six months old, with her next eldest being her brother, her faithful strapper, Stevie, who has Down's syndrome.

'We were the two youngest and grew up together, with a great bond between us, always looking after each other,' she would recount. And look after each other they did, her doing everything she could to see Stevie employed in her trainer's stable, and him working like a trojan to see that his sister's mount was always at its best. You want more?

Okay, we will have that brother do the barrier draw, and pull out the best lane. Number one. Gave her and Prince of Penzance the inside running from the get-go.

As to the race itself, of course, we will have Michelle on Prince of Penzance being well back with 200 metres to go, and then starting to thunder forward, closing on the front-runners as the crowd roars, reeling them in, reeling them in, reeling them in ... and now SURGING forward as the others start to wilt ... to WIN by a head!

We have that! And we have that the first person she wanted to embrace when she got off was not the owner or the trainer, but of course her faithful brother, Stevie.

There is only one thing that can top it all. A fabulously Australian speech where she combined grace and humour with a good gobful of get-that-up-yers to all those who had done her down and doubted whether she and her brother, not to mention their horse, had what it took. Come on, you know you want to hear it again.

'It's such a chauvinistic sport,' she told the Flemington media pack. 'Some of the owners wanted to kick me off the horse, but I thought he had what it takes to run a race in the Melbourne Cup. I can't say how grateful I am to the people who helped me, and I want to say to everyone else—get stuffed. Because women can do anything, and we can beat the world.'

Rah!

And again, I say RAH.

Better story than Phar Lap?

It's a photo finish, and it is the kind of photo that will only be fully developed a decade or two from now, but I am going to call it early.

YES.

Beats Phar Lap by a nose, I tell you!

# C'mon!

If you were in the metaphorical trenches, down to your last bullets, while the enemy had tanks and howitzers aplenty, who would you pick to be with you? It would be hard, surely, to go past Lleyton Hewitt.

Sure, I have had a few goes at him throughout his career, but the one thing that was never at issue was the staggering amount of *fight* he had in him, whatever the position, whatever the odds. Always, even when way behind, when it was obvious to everyone but him that he was going to lose, he still fought on to the last ounce, scratching, biting, fighting like an alley cat for every blessed point.

If there ever was a bloke who deserved to become our Davis Cup captain, it was him.

# World in union

Back in early 2001 when a pioneer gay rugby player by the name of Mark Bingham heard that his gay rugby team—the San Francisco Fog—was to be accepted into the local comp, he wrote an email to his nearest and dearest: 'When I started playing rugby at the age of 16,' he wrote, 'I always thought that my interest in other guys would be an anathema, completely repulsive to the guys on my team and to the people I was knocking the shit out of on the other team. I loved the game, but KNEW I would need to keep my sexuality a secret forever. I feared total rejection.

'As we worked and sweated and ran and talked together this year, I finally felt accepted as a gay man and a rugby player. My two irreconcilable worlds came together.

'Now we've been accepted into the union and the road is going to get harder. We need to work harder. We need to get better. We have the chance to be role models for other gay folks who wanted to play sports but never felt good enough or strong enough. More importantly, we have the chance to show the other teams in the league that we are as good as they are. Good rugby players. Good partiers. Good sports. Good men.

'Gay men weren't always wallflowers waiting on the sideline. We have the opportunity to let these other athletes know that gay men were around all along on their little-league teams, in their classes, being their friends. This is a great opportunity to change a lot of people's minds and to reach a group that might never have had to know or hear about gay people. Let's go make some new friends . . . and win a few games.

'Congratulations, my brothers in rugby.'

Love that. A short time later, Bingham was on United Airlines Flight 93 on September 11 2001, when the passengers realised America was under attack. Bingham, with two other men, Jeremy Glick and Todd Beamer, decided to go down fighting. An operator on a GTE Airfone had a brief conversation with Beamer, in which he told her he knew he was going to die, but asked her to say the Lord's Prayer with him before he started.

She did that, then heard Beamer say to Bingham and Glick: 'Are you guys ready?'

There was a rumbling affirmation, then Beamer said, 'Let's roll.'

Roll they did. Right into the cockpit, and brought the plane down, a long way short of its probable target of the White House.

The operator, Lisa Jefferson, heard the sounds of screaming and scuffling before the line went dead.

These days, the gay rugby World Cup, held every four years, is named the Mark Bingham Cup.

CAUTION
LOMU

# Lomu awesome, that's a fax

I am not sure the rugby world will ever see a more exciting player than Jonah Lomu, the original 'Freight Train in Ballet Shoes'. I will always treasure something Jonah's captain, Sean Fitzpatrick, showed me on the eve of the final of their triumphant 1995 World Cup campaign.

It was a fax sent by an eight-year-old lad from Christchurch:

*Dear All Blacks,*
*Remember, rugby is a TEAM game.*
*All 14 of you, pass the ball to Jonah!*
*Sam*

# A quiet achiever

In February 2016 the National Museum made the wonderful announcement that it had bought Australian Olympian Peter Norman's famous singlet from the 1968 Mexico City Olympics, where Norman was outrageously excoriated, and then rightly celebrated for what happened after he won the silver medal in the 200 metres. Before the medal ceremony, in the changing room, Norman found out that the two black American athletes—gold medallist John Carlos, and bronze medallist Tommie Smith— were about to deliver Black Power salutes in protest at the treatment of black people in America.

'I will stand with you,' Norman said quietly, and he did just that, wearing an Olympic Project for Human Rights badge to indicate his solidarity.

Come the moment, Norman, on the silver podium, was the one nearest the flags and so had his back to the two Americans, but he knew they were proceeding with their plan when . . .

'When I was standing there,' he told me in 1999, 'and I could hear this particularly rich baritone singing *The Star-Spangled Banner*, really belting it out, and then the voice suddenly faded out. I knew then that John and Tommie had gone ahead with it . . .'

The same thing happened all over the stadium, with the singing replaced by stunned silence, which was in short order replaced by cat calls and booing. It was an iconic sporting moment, when our bloke stood on the right side of history—even if, at the time, it was so much thought to be the wrong side that the two Americans were immediately sent home in disgrace. As for Norman, it was strongly asserted that the reason he was not picked for the 1972 Olympics was because of his actions in 1968, though that is hotly disputed by the AOC.

Either way, by 1999, when I interviewed him for a profile piece before the Sydney Games, he proved to be a very inspiring man, who'd nevertheless done it a bit tough in previous years, with alcoholism and depression. He had been all but entirely forgotten by the wider world. But the Americans knew, and honoured him. And his family knew.

Just a week before I talked to him, Norman's young teenage daughter, Emma, was asked by her high school teacher to write a story 'about a famous person'.

'I'd like to write about my father,' Emma said.

'Emma,' the teacher replied, 'it is nice that all children think their parents are famous, but I want an essay about a *really* famous person.'

'Well,' Emma replied equably, 'he's in all five of those sports books you've got on the shelf, so isn't that famous enough?'

Gotcha!

Norman died of a heart attack a decade ago, and both Smith and Carlos gave eulogies and were pallbearers at his funeral. On 11 October 2012, Dr Andrew Leigh guided through the Australian Parliament an official apology which noted, 'That this House: "Acknowledges the bravery of Peter Norman in donning an Olympic Project for Human Rights badge on the podium . . . and apologises . . . for the treatment he received upon his return to Australia, and the failure to fully recognise his inspirational role before his untimely death in 2006".

Bravo, Peter Norman. Bravo the National Museum for honouring him in this manner.

# Diff'rent strokes

It was in the northern autumn of 1973 . . .

The great Australian marathon swimmer Des Renford is exultant. On this, his third crossing of the English Channel, he has left the French shores behind just eight hours ago and can already hear the sound of a foghorn on the English shore ahead. It means that the record for the fastest crossing is practically his, if he could just power through the last mile or so.

And yet, just as Shakespeare once said that *'There is a tide in the affairs of men/Which, if taken at the flood/leads on to fortune,'* so too is it true that it can be very grim indeed for a man when that tide suddenly turns.

For so it is on this occasion, with the current that has been roughly aiding him now continually pushing him sideways, almost like someone has pulled a lever somewhere and he is being flushed down the channel. Renford fights it with everything he has in him. The sun goes down, the moon comes up, and Renford is still out there ploughing on, with his support boat beside him, trying to encourage him to maintain the rage.

Finally, finally though, after another full five hours of this, his hands hit something solid beneath him. The sand, the beach, the English shore. Yesssss!

Renford staggers forward the best he can, out of the water and onto the shore like some primeval creature of ages past. Then he collapses onto the beach as his support staff swing into action.

Cold, very cold. Renford is all but blue with it. Shivering, shaking, wrapped tight in a blanket and grimly trying to keep his mouth open long enough for his trainer to slip some jelly beans in, to give him sustenance. His tongue is so swollen with all the salt water that has been around it that there is only just room to get some of those mashed jelly-beans in and down his throat.

He has landed on a lost shore of Ye Olde England, at a beach called The Coalmine, in the middle of a foggy night, and it really seems as if there is, in all probability, not another soul for miles around.

It was just then, from out of the swirling thick fog, that an Englishman rolls up, walking his Dalmatian dog. Perhaps 60 or so, the fellow looks to have come straight from Central Casting with his tweed jacket, leather patches, Sherlock Holmes cap and expression of benign, oblivious contentedness.

The Englishman looks down at Renford, takes in all the feverish activity around him as they try to bring his body temperature up from the dangerously low level to which it has fallen. Then the man can hold his question in no longer:

'Been swimming, then?'

Renford looks up at the man through eyes squinty with fatigue and disbelief at the question, and slowly nods his head—even as his support staff tries to usher the man away.

The Englishman will not be put off, though, and follows up: 'Innit cold then?' (This, as the support crew are trying to get even more blankets around the Australian, all blue and shuddering.)

Still, Des manages to get out through his chattering teeth a growled 'Bloody freezing'.

It is at this point that one of Renford's men steps in and explains to the local that not only has Renford been swimming, but he has just crossed the English Channel, so perhaps it would be a good idea if the fellow stopped asking him questions and PUSHED OFF!

*Still* the Englishman will not be so easily put off, and reaches down to pat Renford on the head before leaving. 'Jolly good show then,' he says, with another head pat for good measure. Then he disappears off into the fog, never to be seen again.

# Collins class

Jerry Collins, the famed All Blacks No. 6—an heir to Buck Shelford and Zinzan Brooke—once played a game of reserve grade for a village team in Britain, simply because he had been taking some R&R nearby, had been asked, and wanted to help out. He turned out for the Barnstaple Seconds, against Newton Abbott. Certainly Collins dropped back four gears so as not to destroy the game and yet, at one point when the Newton Abbott wing Aidan Tolley was about to score, the ball tucked under his left arm and his right arm raised in celebration, Collins' killer instinct was too strong.

'He didn't see me coming,' Collins told the *Sunday Times*. 'I caught him in the air, faced him the other way and carried him back a few yards. He said, "Damn, it, you could have let me score that." "I couldn't help myself," I said.'

Late in the game, it was one of Barnstaple's props who couldn't help himself. The prop was injured and waiting for a stretcher to remove him, when he noted a concerned Collins standing over him. 'Any chance of a photo, Jerry?' he asked. Collins obliged, lying on the ground by the prop so the photo could be taken.

Once the game was over, Collins didn't just leave, but went back to the clubhouse and got to know his fellow reserve-graders. They bonded further. And Collins took a decision.

'I have asked the Barnstaple guys,' Collins told the *Sunday Times*, 'if it would be OK for me to wear their socks when I play for the Barbarians against South Africa at Twickenham. I have played for the club and it's something I would like to do.'

So the flame of rugby flickers on the way it should, even this far into the professional era. But sadly Jerry Collins and his partner died in the early hours of a Friday morning in an horrific car crash in France in June 2015.

# Cathy's crown

The reporter from Britain's Independent Television Network came straight to the point as the cameras rolled: just why was it so incredibly important to you Australians, Mr FitzSimons, that Cathy Freeman won that gold medal yesterday at the Sydney Olympic Games?

Good question.

I think the answer is that it was important because she was a fantastic Australian athlete, who was good enough to win Olympic gold; because it seemed like her destiny to do so; and because, as Australians, we wanted to see her do it! Rah! Rah! Rah!

It was important, too, because, well beyond all that, we are a nation with a deeply troubled past on the Aboriginal front and at this moment, as a country, we were trying to reconcile that troubled past with a far brighter future. Cathy Freeman was the best known Aboriginal Australian in the land and, in some way, having her blast her way to the top of the podium while we cheered ourselves hoarse—my three-year-old daughter shouting at the TV screen in exultation, 'Go, Taffy! GO, TAFFY'—felt like it helped to hasten the healing.

We'd been following this story for ten years, ever since she burst on to the scene as a 16-year-old kid from Queensland who, after sending away for a How To Run Fast book as a kid, proceeded to win gold at the Auckland Commonwealth Games as her launching pad. We watched her rise from there to prominence purely by constantly winning such a high-octane event as the 400 metres against the best the world could throw at her.

We observed how, from shy beginnings, her confidence grew to the point where she was happy to drape herself in the Aboriginal flag for a victory lap and damn the consequences; how she was able to keep on winning despite such things as a distressing legal suit with a former lover/coach.

After a past like that, the only true perfect ending possible was for her to win an Olympic gold medal on home soil.

Dickens would have wanted it, Banjo Paterson would have wanted it, Spielberg would have wanted it. And we wanted it, dammit!

It was important because she was a sports personality who we really liked—a young woman who some time in the previous few years had gone from simply being Cathy Freeman to the far more intimate 'Our Cathy', and she was no less than the nation's favourite daughter.

If you were to bottle the emotion that Grant Hackett's mum felt when her boy won the 1500 metres at those Games, and compare it with what the nation as a whole felt after Cathy's victory, I reckon they'd show up as being something akin.

It was important because, while it was terrific to see Australia win all those gold medals at our home Games, in all sorts of different fields from shooting to water polo, Freeman's in the 400m felt like a gold medal AAA, perhaps because the country hadn't seen a track gold medal since Debbie Flintoff King won one in the 400m hurdles in 1988.

No, she didn't cure cancer. She didn't alleviate world hunger all on her own. But the way the nation wildly celebrated her Olympic victory was proof positive that we have come a long, long way from the darker days of our past.

# Barassi

In May of 1993 Ron Barassi has just taken over the position as coach of the then rock-bottom Sydney Swans, who are just moments away from playing against Carlton at the Sydney Cricket Ground.

It will be the Swans' first game under the new coach's command, and Barassi softly closes the dressing-room door, sits all his players down, and begins to spin them a tale. He speaks in a low-key, yet strangely emotive voice. 'Imagine,' he says, 'that it's 20 years from now. Imagine the Sydney Swans have now won the flag three years in a row, that they're continuing to break ground records and have more than 100,000 people regularly turning up to games.

'Imagine you're in a bar, somewhere in Sydney, and at the next table someone recognises you,' continues Barassi, 'and they say: "Hey, didn't you used to play for the Swans back in the early '90s? Hang on," they'll say, "weren't you there when they won that really big game—against Carlton or Collingwood, or someone— that turned it all around, won it at a time when things were so grim their whole survival was in question? Wasn't that you there that day?"'

'And men,' says Barassi in the pin-drop dressing-room, 'I want you to imagine what it would be like to be able to say right then and there, "Yes I was there when we turned it around. I played the game against Carlton when out of nowhere the Swans won

and then kept on winning from there. I was a part of that team the day we turned the corner." Men we can do it. It is possible that we can win this game. It's up to you.'

Then the new coach turns on his heel and walks out.

It was a vintage Barassi speech to some totally enthralled footballers, spoiled only by the fact that the newly pumped-up team didn't then go out and wipe their boots all over the fancy-pants schmucks from Carlton and record a victory.

But what the hell? I love that story.

# The rose that rose

When I interviewed the great Australian boxer Lionel Rose twenty years ago at his home in Drouin, Victoria, his most moving story concerned when the flew back to Melbourne after his amazing victory over 'Fighting Harada' in Tokyo, in 1969.

'It was funny,' the Indigenous man from notably humble circumstances said with an oddly whimsical look in his eyes, 'to have left Melbourne for Tokyo with about ten people to see me off, my brothers and cousins mostly, and then to come back to that scene. I was flying economy of course, and when I came off the back of the plane at Essendon airport, I caught sight of these six or seven thousand people out on the tarmac, milling around and shouting.

'I thought, geez, there must be a pop star coming off first-class or something, and I looked over to see who it was . . . when I realised it was *me* they were shouting for. It was wild. Then the procession to the civic reception at the Town Hall, along the packed streets of Melbourne.

'It was when I saw my mum standing calmly and proudly right down there in the front of all those people shouting for her son that I think I kinda lost it . . . I dunno. It was a long way from Jackson's Track.'

# Top fuel

My favourite—all right, my only—Australian motor-racing yarn was told to me by Sir Jack Brabham.

See, in the last Formula One race of the 1959 season at Sebring in Florida, Jack was in the fight of his life with four other drivers—not only to win the race, but to be crowned world champion. And *racing* now. Right from the first lap our Jack kept the hammer down and moved into a forward position, pressing all the way while still trying to take care of his car. 'That was a race where we had really got our act together,' he told me, 'where the car, the engine, the gearbox all came together at the same time and it was all just right for going fast for the whole race.'

So he did. Kept going like the hammers of hell until, with only one lap to go, he was a clear lap ahead of the driver coming second. Four hundred yards out, Brabham knew he had it won, (*putt putt*) knew he'd take the chequered flag, (*putt putt putt*) knew he would be the new heavyweight 'champeen' driver in all the world, (*putt putt putt putt*) knew THAT HE'D RUN OUT OF PETROL.

'I just couldn't believe it,' he recalls. 'But I was still hoping that I'd have enough momentum to get over the line, because I was moving at a fair clip.'

Closer now. Three hundred yards, two hundred, one hundred, eighty, almost stopped now, sixty, fifty . . . STOP. With the world driving championship hanging in the balance and his main

rivals roaring up one lap behind him at the rate of some 180mph, Brabham did what he had to do. He got out and pushed. Other cars were still roaring past, of course, and the wind they created was enough to wobble him on his pins, even as he strained his way forward, but he kept going. Onwards, ever onwards.

With only ten yards to go, Brabham had enough momentum up that the main thing was just to keep steering it straight and out of the way of the continually roaring cars. But the man with the chequered flag had his number all the same—and dropped it, at pretty much the same time as Brabham himself dropped on the tarmac over the finish line in fourth place.

Making like the Pope after a long flight on Garuda Airlines, Brabham lay prone in exhaustion on the track for as long as ten seconds, but was soon lifted to his feet by a cheering crowd clamouring around him and slapping him on the back. Eyes right and all hail the new Formula One driving champion of all the world.

On ya, Sir Jack.

# Bobby Pearce

If it wasn't the most heart-warming episode ever in Australian Olympic history, it would have to run close . . .

In the quarterfinals of the sculling competition at the 1928 Amsterdam Olympics, Bobby Pearce, from the famed Pearce family down at Sydney's Spit, was rowing powerfully against the Frenchman, Savrin. He had the wind in his hair, the sun on his back, and every prospect of recording another impressive win. Then he heard it . . .

Even through his rhythmic and stylish exertion and the sound of his own roaring breathing, he could distinguish an added edge to the roar of the crowd lining the banks up ahead. Risking a quick gander, he turned his head and immediately saw what they were on about.

There, about 40 metres away and right in his path—but not in Savrin's—was Mother Duck and perhaps six little ducklings, who had chosen that very moment to go for their late morning constitutional.

The Australian didn't hesitate. One can't actually hit the brakes while sculling, but he did do the next best thing, which was to let his oars linger in the water to slow his boat down, and so allow the family of ducks safe passage.

He then resumed his powerful strokes, and went on to win the race. After he received the gold medal, he was warmly commended by all and sundry for his very humane and compassionate gesture. The kids of Amsterdam, particularly, took him to their heart and followed him around for the rest of the games as if he was the Pied Piper.

The story has a postscript. Some sixty odd years after the event, when Bobby had already been in his grave for at least two decades—he lived until 1976—a member of his family added one small detail to this well-loved story.

'Father was a sympathetic and humane person,' Olympic historian Harry Gordon quoted Pearce's son, Rupert, as saying. 'But he was extremely competitive. If the race had been close, he would have gone right through those ducks like a Mac truck.'

# Our greatest runner up

Ron Clarke, the great Australian distance runner—and late-life politician as mayor of the Gold Coast—first came to international public attention during the 1956 Melbourne Olympics when he was given the enormous honour of lighting the flame in the Olympic cauldron to formally begin the Games. Though he didn't actually compete in those Games, he went on to a great career, notwithstanding the fact that his peaks—standing out like the Himalayas—fitted neatly right between the 1960, 1964 and 1968 Olympics, and his troughs bang on them. Famously, he never did win an Olympic gold, despite being perhaps the greatest long distance runner of his era.

In June 1966, Clarke was invited to an athletic meeting in Prague by Emil Zatopek, the great Czech distance runner of the 1950s. Zatopek was to distance runners what Sir Edmund Hillary was to mountaineering—the first man through the barriers for all the others to follow—and he had long been an admirer of Clarke's style. After the meeting, the four-time Olympic gold medallist and national hero, guided the young Australian around Prague for the day, showing him fine hospitality throughout, talking about this and that, and the art of running in particular.

That afternoon, the Czech champion took Clarke to the airport, took him past the guards, right up the steps of the plane, before warmly shaking his hand and pressing a tiny package into his palm and whispering a few words. What the . . . ? Zatopek

was gone. The plane door closed on him, and Clarke was more than passing nervous. What on earth had Zatopek just given him? Was it drugs? Was it contraband? Was it some sort of message or something he had to take to the free world? Microfilm maybe? Clarke sat in his seat, perspiring a little. He determined that under no circumstances would he open the small package until he was back on the ground in London. At least on friendly, familiar territory, where he would be able to cope with whatever it was.

But somewhere over the English Channel he could resist no longer. Looking surreptitiously over his left and right shoulder to see no-one was watching, he fished the package out of his pocket and opened up the little box inside. It gleamed back at him. It was an Olympic gold medal, the very same that Zatopek had won in the 10,000 metres at the 1952 Helsinki Olympics. It was even newly inscribed, To Ron Clarke, 19 July 1966, with Zatopek's final words on the plane steps coming to him, 'Not out of friendship, but because you deserve it.'

Bravo, Ron Clarke. You bloody well did.

# Goolagong Dreamtime

Way back when Evonne Goolagong first came to herself, she was a little girl being rocked back and forth in the arms of her mother to the sound of singing, beside the river near Condobolin. Her father was on the guitar, while her brothers and sisters, cousins, uncles, aunts, et al., were around the campfire melodically moving with the tune. In the Wiradjuri language, *glagalang* means 'big mob', which is what they were, and happy to be so. Her people had been in these parts for around 40,000 years, she was *of* the land, and not merely living on it, the way her people told it.

'I started hitting against walls when I was six,' she told me in her Noosa home, when I interviewed her, 'and that was from seeing my older sister and brother do it. My dad used to cut out apple-crate boards for handles, and we would just have a ball, no hair on it whatsoever.'

Her dad was Kenny Goolagong, known as one of the hardest-working shearers in the district; her mother was the outgoing and loquacious Linda; and with her seven siblings, Evonne was part of the only Aboriginal family in that lost, tiny town of NSW that is Barellan. Only 15 kilometres or so from the very middle of nowhere, her horizons extended not far further than the wheat fields all around.

Soon—in scenes uncannily reminiscent of the young Donald Bradman hitting golf balls with a single cricket stump in the darkening light of his parents' Bowral farm—the young Evonne graduated from the apple-crate boards to using a broom stick on the hairless balls. 'It was exciting,' she recalled, 'and it made me more determined to do it. I developed my own little game.'

Like Bradman, that game was to hit the ball against the wall as many as times as possible without missing. 'Only on the first bounce,' she recalled with a laugh. 'Two bounces didn't count, and at the end of the day I would write the amount in the ground—deep enough so that it would not be blown away overnight, and then I would come back and try and better that score the next day.'

Other events in her young life brought home to her and the Barellan community that she was also possessed of great athletic ability. 'I remember going to a school athletics day,' she says, 'where you won threepence if you came second, or sixpence if you came first, and I had a whole ten shillings when I came back. I was so excited I walked all the way from the showground, and went and hit on the wall.'

Goolagong dreaming: 'Around then I read a schoolgirl's magazine called *Princess*, about a story of a lady who found this young girl and trained her and became her guardian, and took her to this place called Wimbledon, and that's when I first heard of Wimbledon. I didn't know where Wimbledon was and I thought, "Wow, I would love to go and play at that place", so every time I went back on the wall I would think of that, and I would dream about it . . .'

Soon, the word of her prowess spread so far she was taken to Sydney for proper coaching and, after winning more and more junior tournaments, and attracting ever more attention, she became progressively more conscious of both her ability and her Aboriginality.

The great Indigenous boxer, Lionel Rose, had something to do with that. 'I was in Sydney and I saw him on TV [getting an award],' Evonne recalls, 'and I thought, "Wow", because at that stage I was the only Aboriginal tennis player, a real novelty really. I felt very proud to see him, and I thought, "Well, if he can do it, I can do it".'

She wrote Rose a fan letter, he wrote back, and the young tennis player was even more encouraged. 'He inspired me,' she says simply. Bit by bit it all started to come together, before it *all* came together in a rush!

So much so that by June of 1971, when she was still only nineteen years old, Goolagong was not only at Wimbledon, but in the final against the Australian great, Margaret Court ... while Barellan held its breath.

When 'Our Evonne' took the first set, the folks back home breathed for the first time in thirty minutes and let out a mighty cheer. And when she was leading 5-1 in the second set, Linda turns to look at her husband. 'I think she's going to win it,' he says quietly.

Court to serve, facing match point against her. Her first ball hits the net. 'Now, if she hits this next one into the net,' Kenny Goolagong explains to Linda, 'Evonne's won it ... She did! She did!'

People rush about hugging and laughing. Evonne's father is handed a beer and keeps repeating, starry-eyed, 'Beaut, just beaut!'

A great tennis career was truly launched, and Evonne of course, would go on to win Wimbledon again, a decade later, this time as a happily married mother of a three-year-old.

# Why sport needs more stories like Eddie the Eagle

The film *Eddie the Eagle*, which stars our own Hugh Jackman, is terrific. As a work of fiction it would be fabulous: sort of 'Rocky with coke-bottle glasses, on skis'. But it's all the stronger because it's true. There really *is* an Eddie Edwards, from Gloucestershire in England, who really *did* dream of representing Great Britain in the Winter Olympics, entirely untroubled by the fact that he had precisely no talent whatsoever to genuinely compete in a world class event, and all he had to offer was phenomenal courage.

And, he really did get to the Calgary Winter Olympics where, as I described not long afterwards, he 'launched himself down the ski jump at Calgary, soared like a stone and landed right on the world's funny bone'.

In a Winter Olympics that were long on technical wizardry and short on personality, Eddie became an instant media star like they just don't make them any more.

Amid all the strutting Finns and Swedes, the Austrians and Italian racers who had taken snow with their mother's milk, here was a fellow who looked—with the greatest respect—like the stereotypical last bloke left against the gym wall when the two class captains pick their sides for the PE class practice basketball match. And while the Europeans all had sponsorship and government money behind them, he'd had no support from

anyone and was, in fact, living in a Finnish mental hospital to save money while training, and working as a plasterer to pay for it when informed that he had actually qualified for the Games.

What's more, this was a sport of life and death, of going to the top of the 70-metre ski jump and then the 90-metre ski jump and launching yourself into space at such speed that a single mis-calculation could likely put you into a wheelchair for life.

Abigail van Buren of *Dear Abby* fame once advised 'never engage in a sport that has an ambulance waiting at the finish line', and in this case, Eddie Edwards could look down and see several of them.

'Aren't you scared at the top of the 90-metre jump?' he had been asked.

'Of course I'm scared,' Eddie had replied quite sincerely. 'But I used to be *really* scared.'

Grasping on to that tiny shred of solace, he took a deep breath, launched himself anyway . . . and landed . . . safely!

Sure, he came stone motherless last in both events, but it didn't matter. The world loved him for his courage alone, for the fact that he actually lived his dream. And so fascinated were we all that from the moment one of the journalists gave him the perfect tag 'Eddie the Eagle' his fame kept soaring and soaring, long after the Finns, Swedes, Austrians and Italians had come back to earth. As it happens, he is still soaring nigh on three decades later, while they are long forgotten.

He came out to Australia a few months later, in July 1988, and gave a press conference, which I attended. When I asked him why he thought he had become such a world superstar, he was frank.

'It was not so much because I lost, but rather because I brought some colour to the sport,' he said. 'I think I opened everybody's eyes as to how professional sport is nowadays ... Then, all of a sudden I come along and show everybody what it should be—fun.'

Bingo. We loved Eddie the Eagle because of his courage, yes, and his personal backstory, but mostly because he reminded us of what sport was meant to be about in the first place. Fun. Participation. Having a go!

We loved 'Eric the Eel'—the fellow from Equatorial Guinea who clocked 1 minute 52 seconds for his 100-metre heat—for just the same reasons at the 2000 Olympic Games. Eric the Eel, looked more like a mobile drowner than a swimmer, but for sheer pluck, for the fun of the story, they don't come much better.

And of course the rules have been changed to prevent more Eddies or Erics making the big time—MUCH better to stay with humourless automatons—but it is a mistake.

# Sportsmanship blossoms

Listen, maybe you had to be there—or be to the oval-ball born—to recognise the purity of the rugby moment, but let's go with it anyway. It's September 2015 and at the end of the most stunning match in the history of the World Cup, when the once lowly rugby nation of Japan, with one victory to its credit in 24 World Cup outings over three decades, took on the two-time World Champion Springboks and . . . BEAT the brutes, 34-32, it was a close call as to who was more stunned.

Was it the gobsmacked, diminutive Japanese fans of their national team, the 'Brave Blossoms', barely daring to believe what had just happened, the sheer *joy* of it all? Or the huge, dazed and dejected South Africans, in their green Springboks jerseys, scarcely comprehending how their boys could have been so beaten?

Inevitably, emotions are high both ways. As they leave the Brighton stadium in southern England, the two large masses of the opposing fans suddenly come face to face. They are different peoples, from different parts of the planet, with few intersecting points other than their common humanity, and love of the oval ball.

In other sports, at other times, riots have broken out on such occasions. But, no . . .

Suddenly, four Springbok fans form a guard of honour for the Japanese fans to walk through. And now four more, join.

And now a dozen! And now dozens more! In short, there are two long lines of huge South Africans in Bok jerseys clapping and cheering as the stunned Japanese, gripping their flags, make their way through, many of them crying and pausing only to shake hands and briefly bow before many of those cheering.

Very, very rugby.

# ONLY IN AUSTRALIA

*'Bevo? It's Robbo. How's the situation with Rummo affecting the team?'*
Goodo, and that was a sports quote classico of our time. For that, ladies and gentleman, was Gavin Robertson interviewing Michael Bevan on Sydney radio on what effect Graeme Rummans's failed drugs test would have on the NSW cricket team.

*'This has been the worst year of my life. First, 9/11, and now this.'*
Letter writer to *The Age* after Kangaroos star Wayne Carey left the team when an affair with a team-mate's wife was exposed.

*'Those memories will forever be etched in the tattoo I've got.'*
Jamie Soward reminiscing on his time winning a premiership with the Dragons. Hallmark greeting cards, eat your freaking HEARTS out!

*'And Australian Rules . . . where did that come from? Is it that we live so f--king far from anywhere, we can just make shit up!?'*
The late, great Robin Williams, doing an impromptu stand-up routine at Sydney's Sugarmill Hotel in 2010.

*'Australia was started as a penal colony in the beginning. They went on to become patriotic Australians, got their own accent, moved away from the British and here we are.'*

American tennis player Venus Williams' summation of our country on Australia Day.


*'The haka doesn't really impress me much. I grew up in a bedroom with six brothers, so I grew up seeing that kind of thing on a daily basis.'*

Glen Ella, speaking at a rugby lunch.

# His mate swam *towards* the shark

It was one of the most extraordinary episodes in Australian sport.

There was Australian surfing champion Mick Fanning bobbing in the surf at Jeffreys Bay in South Africa as the JBay Open Surfing Championship was being broadcast live to the world. And we viewers could see something that Mick couldn't. It was a big bloody shark fin, clearly attached to a big bloody shark coming at him from behind!

And now, just as the shark reaches him, the wave rises, obscuring our view for a good ten seconds. Former world champion Martin Potter, commentating live on TV, speaks for everyone at home, too, when he can't help himself and says: 'Oh, f--k . . .'

Is Mick Fanning being savaged as we speak? The world leans forward and waits for the wave to ebb, so we can see again and . . .

And there he is! ALIVE!

But the shark is still coming at him.

Two things happen. First Mick does the obvious—no, really—and *punches* the shark, trying to beat the beggar back. Meantime, Fanning's fellow competitor, Queenslander Julian Wilson, is about ten metres away.

Did someone say a fellow Australian is in trouble? 'Mick was looking at me,' Wilson would recount, 'when a big old fish popped up behind him. It was a lot bigger than him. I saw him

start to get kind of manhandled by the shark and I was kind of freaking out.'

But he had to do, what he had to do: 'He was kind of getting wrestled off his board and then a wave came between us and I started paddling for him, just fearing for his life . . . I was like, "I've got a board, if I can get there I can stab it or whatever, I've got a weapon".'

In Australia, the mothers of both Fanning and Wilson are watching, live, petrified. Mick Fanning's mother, Elizabeth Osborne, later recalled: 'I was absolutely terrified. I went over to the television almost as though I could pull him out . . . to save him. I couldn't believe what I was seeing. I thought we'd lost him.'

The wave comes again, obscuring both surfers, as the world waits, not daring to breathe, and . . .

And there they are! Wilson has got him. Outnumbered, smacked, the shark turns and takes off, and in short order the men on the jet-ski arrive to grab both surfers. The day is saved.

Later, that evening, still incredulous, Fanning and his surfing mates—including Wilson, his brother for life—get together to have a few drinks, and talk it over. 'There was about eight grown men in there,' Fanning would recount, 'and every single one of us was crying. There was a lot of love and relief, but it was so strange though . . . It felt like I was at my own wake, to be honest. I got some sleep but it was a pretty restless night.'

Beyond Fanning and his immediate circle, the surfing world, and much of the world itself, can talk of little else. 'Those shots of him swimming?', another Australian surfing champion Barton Lynch is quoted as saying. 'Then turning around to see if it is coming for him? That's life and death, literally. You don't see that in many sports. It makes tennis and golf look pretty bloody boring.' Indeed.

But, all's well that ends well. Three days later, both surfers are back in Australia, with their mothers there to greet them at the airport. 'All we have to do,' Wilson's mother Noela told my wife Lisa Wilkinson on the *Today Show*, 'is be grateful that they're both coming home with all their bits . . .'

# Hit for six

Jonathan Agnew and Kerry O'Keeffe were the ABC co-commentators on the occasion of the famous Steve Waugh innings at the SCG in the fifth Test against the English in January 2003. On the last ball of the day, Waugh was on 96, their conversation went like this.

Agnew: Well what high drama we have here Kerry. What will he do?

K O'K: He'll go for it.

JA: But he could come back tomorrow and wait for a trundler down the leg side . . .

K O'K: Stuff tomorrow Aggers, tomorrow is for silver medallists. We're Australians. Poms come back tomorrow. Australians only want the gold and we want it now . . .

Whereupon Waugh, indeed, sent the final ball flying for four!

# Special K

The scene was set at the end of a long day at the Australian Open in Melbourne in January 2001. Standing at the head of a queue of tired players waiting to return to their hotels in the courtesy cars is Our Pat, and one of the limos swings in to pick him up. Suddenly, though, a queue-jumping Anna Kournikova appears and slides into the back seat.

She is about to tell the driver where to go when the door opens and there is Pat Rafter with the sparkle of high dudgeon in his eyes, looking ready to tell her where to go. Gently, though, he tells 'Special K' just where the back of the queue is, and even points it out to her so she will have no trouble finding the way.

This is the way we do things in Australia. Suitably embarrassed, Kournikova has no choice but to cede the car to Rafter, move to the back of the queue and wait like everyone else.

The small band of spectators who witnessed the scene apparently loved every moment of it. As you would.

# Patty Mills for PM!

What a story, that of Patty Mills. His father is a Torres Strait Islander, his mother of the Ynunga Nation in South Australia and, raised in Canberra, he began playing b'ball with an Indigenous team his parents started, The Shadows, and starred from the first. 'But still so slight and weedy, one would doubt his power to stay . . .'

At only 1.83 metres fully grown, surely he couldn't really make it in the big time? Think again, after a circuitous route he made it all the way to the San Antonio Spurs. In June 2014 and last Monday (AEST) in the fifth match of NBA finals against Le Bron James' Miami Heat, it was Mills who in the third quarter nailed five from eight three-pointers to help push his team over the top so they became the national champions. He was so dominant that ESPN commentators gave American viewers an impressive lesson in Indigenous Australian history, including the triumph of Eddie Mabo launching his action to secure Aboriginal land rights.

At the match's end, Mills covered himself in the Torres Strait Island flag in honour of his father.

'It's Australian history and we are proud of it,' Mills said afterwards, of ESPN's commentary, and the flag, 'to educate people not just in Australia but overseas was the next level. To use pro basketball to help educate people on our culture is something I've always tried to do—so to have it come off like that was special.'

# Military tactics

In the early 80s, playing league for the mighty Stanley Rivers Rugby League Club, Brisbane Fitzphile Michael Clifford and his mates found themselves in a social match against the Moreton Bay Pub side, which was owned at the time by the great Arthur Beetson.

Although well and truly retired from professional football by this time, and terribly unfit, Artie played in this game, see, and was his usual devastating self in the first half. Watch now as, in typical style, each time he gets the ball he draws in three or four frantic defenders, before effortlessly offloading to set up his team mates. He is *destroying* them.

At half time, however, the Stanley Rivers coach, Joey Chambers, brings his players in tight and, with a gleam in his eye, tells them quietly: 'When he gets the ball next time, just let him go through.'

Sure enough, early in the second half, near his own line, Artie gets the ball. Stanley Rivers players, just like Scipio's soldiers, step aside. Artie, like Hannibal's elephants, charges through. He runs three-quarters of the field before, pale and puffing like a sick rhinoceros in the desert, his legs start to wobble and, exhausted, he is cut down.

And that, friends. is the end of Artie, who has to leave the field for want of breath! Genius, coach.

# All in the family

When Brett Voss, playing for St Kilda, was lining up for a critical goal late in a game against Akermanis' Brisbane Lions, the man in front of Voss trying to put him off was none other than his older brother Michael Voss.

Just as Brett had composed himself and was about to commence his run, the older Voss piped up: 'My dad's slept with your mum!'

It was true. It was undeniable. And Brett missed.

Rather more pointedly, so far as family sledges are concerned, there was the occasion when Dean Waugh—a highly accomplished cricketer in his own right—was having a rare bad day with the bat, and was constantly missing delivery after delivery, only for the bowler to finally stop mid-pitch, put his hands on his hips, and ask: 'Mate, are you sure you're not adopted?'

# Quick quiz

Who was the first English captain to tour both Australia and New Zealand, and return home without scoring a single run or taking a single wicket?

*(Answer over page. No peeking, until you have had a real go.)*

Who was the first... both Australia and
New Zealand... single run or
taking a...

# Quiz answer

The only English captain to have toured both Australia and New Zealand, and return home without taking a wicket or scoring a run is . . . Captain Cook!

Thank you, thank you all! I am here till Thursday. Try the veal!

# The kick that stopped a nation

It was a Saturday afternoon in 2001, see, and Oatley RSL soccer team was playing Sans Souci in a notably tense last-round match of their competition at Renown Park in Oatley, the same ground where the great Reg Gasnier once honed his fabulous skills. The scores are locked, as the minutes tick away, and the crowd is on the edge of their proverbials . . .

The ball goes out of bounds. Throw-in to be taken. The laddie is about to throw the ball in, when suddenly he stops stock still.

What is it? The crowd hoots, but the lad doesn't move. He's just heard something from the bench, which in turn has been listening to ABC radio: *'Ealesy's lining up a penalty to win the match, the ref's blown full-time.'*

Meantime, the ref at Oatley calls: 'Throw it in! I'll book you if you don't stop wasting time!'

The thrower calls back what he's just heard. The ref, master of the occasion, takes immediate action, and blows his whistle for 'time off'. Both sides rush to the sideline to hear the call.

The kick goes through! Australia have won! The Bledisloe Cup is ours! Back at Oatley, pandemonium. Both sides start high-fiving. After nearly ninety minutes of close struggle, guys who'd been marking each other fiercely, now embrace warmly.

Even the ref can't stop smiling and also momentarily loses his distant reserve by whooping it up with the players and his linesmen. At last he blows 'time on again' and the teams play on.

As good as it gets!

# Way to go Buddha

Gargantuan former Wallaby prop Chris 'Buddha' Handy was in
the backblocks of Queensland, about to get on a light plane back
to Brissie after a speaking gig.

'How much do you weigh?' the Rex Airlines person behind
the counter asked.

'Why?' Buddha asked.

'We need to know how much petrol to put in the plane.'

'I'm 250 kilos! FILL IT UP!'

———

A good man, Buddha, even if he and I had a mild dispute for a
while as to which of us could claim the title of the heaviest man
ever to walk across the Kokoda Track. In my own gargantuan
days I did the track with a starting weight of 132 kilograms, and
was firm in the view that, if Buddha really was heavier than that,
he simply couldn't have done it.

Three things convinced me I was wrong.

Firstly, once I talked to Buddha face-to-face, he was clearly
sincere that he really was in the mid-130 kilogram range when
he did it.

Secondly, I talked to blokes who walked it with him, who were
still in awe as to how he would start two hours ahead of them in
the wee hours of the morning, and finish a couple of hours after
them, and never complain.

Thirdly, those blokes told me a story I will always treasure. That is, before Buddha's trek started, the native porters—heirs to the famed 'Fuzzy-Wuzzy Angels' of World War II, as the Diggers referred to them with deep respect—handed Buddha a silver shovel to carry.

'What's this for?' Buddha asked.

A stream of Pidgin English was the reply.

Translated, they told him: 'We're here to tell you, big boy, if you drop dead, we ain't carrying you out!'

Breakfast of Champions

# Rust never sleeps

Channel Ten commentator Greg Rust to race driver Garth Tander the day before the Bathurst 1000: 'So how do you prepare for the big race? What will you be doing tonight?'

Tander to Rust: 'You go to bed, mate. Then you get up, have breakfast and go in the race.'

# We few, we happy few

You have to imagine the scene. It was Saturday night at the rollicking Gladesville Hotel and the rugby club of St Ignatius Old Boys were in the midst of celebrating a very successful outing in the semi-finals of the sub-district rugby competition at Ryde International Oval.

Presently, one of the Old Ignatians, a certain Rob Keogh, took the stage and called for quiet. Begging the crowd's indulgence, he recalled the Battle of Agincourt, recounted in Shakespeare's *Henry V*. Immediately before they took on the 25,000 French soldiers, the young king addresses his 5000 to give them mettle.

At the Gladesville pub, Keogh assumed the role of Henry V himself, and drew certain parallels with the Iggies' club and their forthcoming grand final. It went like this:

*This season shall be the feast of Ignatians:*
*He that outlives this year, with limbs intact,*
*Will stand a tip-toe at the millennium's birth,*
*And rouse him at the name of Old Ignatians.*
*He that shall play this game, and see old age,*
*Will yearly on the finals' vigil feast his neighbours,*
*And say, 'To-morrow be the final round.'*
*Then will he strip his sleeve, and show his scars.*
*And say 'These wounds I had on finals' day'.*
*Old men forget: yet all shall be forgot,*

*But he'll remember, with advantages,*
*What feats he did that day: then shall our names,*
*Familiar in his mouth as household words,*
*Sir Dart, Maso, Elvis, Ando, The*
*Oracle, Timo, Stace & Shogo,*
*The list be long and honourable,*
*Be in their flowing cups freshly remember'd.*
*This story shall the good man teach his son;*
*And the Bruce Graham Shield shall ne'er go by,*
*From this day to the ending of the world,*
*But we in it shall be remember'd;*
*We few, we happy few, we band of brothers.*
*For he that plays this game with me*
*Shall be my brother; be he ne'er so vile,*
*This game shall gentle his condition.*
*And gentlemen of rugby with lesser heart,*
*Shall think themselves accursed they were not here;*
*And hold their manhoods cheap, whiles any speaks*
*That fought with us upon this club championship year.*

As you'd expect, the reaction was roaring applause from the forwards, each of whom appreciated the finer points of The Bard's immortal words. Of course, it was met with stupefaction from the backs, who had some vague recollection that this fellow Shakespeare might once have played on the wing for England, but that's about as far as it went.

# Great man rose to the occasion

Well after his Olympic career was over, Murray Rose was back in Australia and surfing at Manly Beach in rough conditions when he couldn't help but notice that a very old bloke was staying with him on every wave. Time and again, amazingly, the old bloke wouldn't drop off.

Finally, when they got to the shore on the same wave, the old bloke looked at him and said: 'Aren't you Murray Rose?'

'Yes, I am,' he replied.

'I'm Boy Charlton,' the old bloke replied. 'Let's crack another one.'

And so they did, all afternoon! Murray told me it was one of his most cherished swimming memories.

# Lines out

In 2007, I attended the funeral of the Wallaby great Trevor Allan, and was moved by a small episode that occurred when the moment came to carry his casket into the chapel at Northern Suburbs Crematorium. His coffin was to be borne by members of the 1948 Wallabies side he so gloriously captained, and as the old men with cauliflower ears milled about at the back of the hearse, it was clear they were a tad unsure as to who should do what, how they should position themselves.

'Gentlemen,' said the undertaker, taking the matter in hand, 'line yourself up like a short lineout, and we'll put Mr Allan down the middle.'

Things were sorted out within seconds, and the flying centre was borne high on the shoulders of the Wallaby forwards once more as in days of yore.

—

A scene poignantly reminiscent of this took place at the same crematorium years later, at the funeral of Daniel Vickerman. Under the tragic circumstances, the coffin his former teammates were so deeply honoured to be asked to bear was always going to be a heavy load—both emotionally and physically. Milling at the back of the hearse, Brendan Cannon, Richard Bell, Jeanot Boutry, David Lyons, Chris Malone and David Fitter were also momentarily unsure as to who should do what.

'Which end is the heaviest?' Brendan Cannon asked the undertaker, who indicated it was the front of the coffin. Right, then.

'Canno and I will take the heavy load,' breathed David Fitter, former Wallaby prop and tight-head of the famed Sydney University 2005 premiership-winning side with Cannon as hooker and Daniel Vickerman, the pillar of the pack, the one who locked between them.

'Canno,' Fitter continued, 'you go left, I will go right side, and for one last time we can have the "Big V" between us.'

And so it went as they quickly lined up accordingly, with the others in tight behind. The once immoveable right side of the scrum of the triumphant Varsity team of 2005 was complete once more, with the warrior borne to his rest on the shoulders of his brethren.

We weep.

# Yeah, nah? Nah, yeah

A few years ago, I noted the rule posted on Twitter that maintained that: 'You Know You're Australian when you understand intuitively that "nah, yeah" means yes and "yeah, nah" means no.'

The best variant ever was the one given by Josh Mansour when he was asked by Channel Nine's Danny Weidler whether being made a Kangaroo so suddenly from out of the blue, and so young, made him reflect on all the work he had put in to get to this point?

'Yeah, nah, ah definitely,' Mansour memorably replied.

On balance, and upon consultation, here is the translation:

'Yeah Danny, it has made me reflect on all that work. Nah, I don't want to sound immodest, so I am throwing in a "nah" in order to not be seen to be too quickly agreeing with the generous praise contained in your question. But ah—another pause to show modest hesitation—definitely, when I think about it, you got me dead to rights, and I definitely did work bloody hard to achieve this honour and I really have reflected on that fact.'

Case solved.

# Johns the ineffable

Rugby league brouhahas don't come much bigger than the time that Andrew Johns looked touch judge Matt Cecchin right in the eye, and expressed in his own manner, the displeasure he felt that the touchie had made a decision that Johns disagreed with.

'F--k you, c--t!' said Johns.

The result was endless hand-wringing and hoo-ha with all of us with access to typewriters and microphones decrying the sad state of sportspeople today.

It took John Singleton to put a stop to it, by simply stepping forward and, with typical cut-through, having the last word on the saga: 'Anyone who doesn't say f--k and c--t shouldn't be allowed to play rugby league.'

Thank you, Your Honour, the defence rests!

# 'F--k it!'

Lyn Deegan was playing in a ladies' competition at Bowral Golf Club when she couldn't help but notice that one of her playing partners was becoming so impatient with anything less than a perfect shot that she kept muttering loudly, 'F' it!' . . . 'F' it!'

By the third hole this was becoming too much for Lyn, who suggested to her partner that if it would make her feel better she should let it all out, and scream out just once 'F--- it!'—as in using all four letters of the 'F' word.

Came the icy reply: 'My dear, I was saying: 'Effort, effort!'

# When the Diggers stumped the Turks

It was undoubtedly the most extraordinary game of cricket played. History records not a jot of who batted, bowled or fielded, nor even whether there was a result, but its extra-ordinariness relies on nothing as trivial as the score. It was where it was played that counts, and in what circumstances.

Gallipoli, December 1915. The battle had been lost, the struggle foregone. General Kitchener gave the orders to pull the Anzacs out and send them on to the Western Front in France. Under cover of darkness, the evacuation began on 8 December. Over the next 11 nights, 35,445 men were safely evacuated on to the ships, suffering only one minor casualty in the process.

As the ranks begin to noticeably thin, it is decided that something should be done to alleviate whatever suspicions Johnny Turk might be harbouring about the decreased activity. The orders go out from First Division command that each battalion is to be as active as possible within sight of the Turks, primarily to create the impression that these visible men are the tip of the iceberg of the troops still in the trenches (many of whom have since departed).

Each battalion is to interpret these commands as it sees fit. Many choose to have men loitering about, gazing at the sky, just beyond the range of the enemy guns. Some men from New South Wales 4th Battalion have other ideas, though. Why not a cricket game? (Apart from mortar and rifle fire from the trenches above, that is.) The relationship between the Turks and the Anzacs have evolved by this time to the point where taking potshots at distant figures is not absolutely automatic but, on the other hand, the departing hospital ships are full of diggers who have trusted this line of reasoning too far.

It is a tentative group therefore who, on the afternoon of 17 December, set foot onto the pockmarked patch of ground known as Shell Green (so named because it is under permanent Turkish artillery fire). The Turks in the trenches above must be wondering what on earth is going on as the game starts. Is this grenade-throwing practice? Or perhaps a method of whacking incoming grenades back to the trenches whence they came?

Who knows what they think, but for the first two hours of the game the Turks hold their fire and watch. But after two or three hours the Turks have had enough of this strange spectacle, and start to send down some mortar fire to clear the Australians out.

The Turks probably still didn't know what was happening, but wanted whatever it was stopped. Did the mortar fire stop the cricket cold? Not bloody likely. According to the diary of one Granville Ryrie, quoted in Bill Gammage's book *The Broken Years*, the game continued anyway, 'just to let them see we were quite unconcerned . . . and when shells whistled by we pretended to field them. The men were wonderfully cheerful and seemed to take the whole thing as a huge joke.'

'The shrapnel cut and hissed across the pitch and the outfield,' the Australian War Memorial chronicles, 'and there was as great a risk of lost life as a lost ball.'

When the Australians still didn't retire, the Turks unleashed doubly heavy salvos of mortar fire and, to use Gammage's phrase, 'the Australians reluctantly called it a draw and retired to tea'.

Happily, there is no record of any player having to 'retire hurt', or worse, during the game.

Two days later, all players were safely evacuated to either be killed on the fields of France or to survive and make it home—home to Australia.

Shell Green now serves as a cemetery for fallen Anzacs.

# Gazumping the moon

Everyone who is now nudging fifty or older knows where they were and what they were doing on the day that Neil Armstrong set foot on the moon.

Back in 1999, on the occasion of the thirtieth anniversary of that momentous event, my then sports editor at the *Sydney Morning Herald* told me his own story . . .

As he recounted, he was at Bowral a couple of hours drive south of Sydney, furiously fiddling with the nobs on the car radio, trying to pick up a radio station carrying the live broadcast.

Finally he got on to Radio 2KY, the great Sydney and Australian horse-racing station, and had tuned in just in time to hear Armstrong utter those immortal words: 'That's one small step for man, one giant leap for . . .'

*'Rrrrracing now at Moruya!'*

# A leap of faith

She was a nice woman, and she told me a story.

One of her best friends is a Catholic priest, see, and a few Sundays ago he was filling in at a Sydney parish church for one of his brother priests who was on sick leave. As he began to administer the sacrament of Holy Communion, two queues, which included a lot of elderly nuns, were shuffling forward towards him down the main aisle, heading for their bread and wine, when a shadow fell across him and he looked up. Four back on the right, was John Eales.

'And at that moment,' he recounted to my informant, 'I could only wish I had had a rugby ball. Because I really think we could have won that lineout!'

# Winners only

One of my spies was at a Swans v West Coast game at the SCG, sitting behind an eight-year-old boy sitting between his father and grandfather. The whole lot of them looked to be West Coast supporters, to judge by the scarves they wore. During most of the game the two men were talking up the Eagles to the boy, telling him how well the Eagles were playing and initially by how much they were in front.

Alas, as the momentum of the game changed and the Swans hit the lead, the focus also moved, with 'We're only two goals behind', 'We need the next four goals straight' and 'We can still do it'.

With about ten minutes to go, the father said: 'If we don't score next, son, I'm afraid that we might not be able to catch up.'

With that, the boy turned to his dad and said: 'That's OK, Dad, but now can I put on my Swans scarf?'

He did, and was proudly draped in it for the rest of the game, happy as Larry.

Gosh, darn it, that's the spirit this country was built on!

# Bob the Barbarian

Roy Masters tells the story of how the famously bookish NSW premier Bob Carr once boasted at a Monday morning Cabinet meeting that he had attended a football game the previous day.

When asked whether it was rugby union or rugby league that he had watched, the premier fired back: 'Don't ask trick questions.'

# The Don

Cricket aficionados will remember the particularity of the West Indies Test team of the 1980s, centring around its selection policy. See, while most Test sides would pick two or three fast bowlers in every side, it was a point of honour with the West Indies to pick *eleven* fast bowlers, and even then they weren't done. They also picked a twelfth man who was a fast bowler, the manager, Wes Hall, was a fast bowler, the bus driver, a bloke called Joey, was a fast bowler. They were a side that *believed* in fast bowling.

And so it was that on a hot summer's day at the Adelaide Oval in January of 1987, when the young Mervyn Hughes went out to face the might of the West Indies pace attack, no one was expecting him to last long. Maybe not even Merv did. But what he did know is that whatever else, he would go down swinging, and with that in mind he opened his mighty shoulders and started thrashing lustily at every ball that came his way, in the classic 'have a go, ya mug' Australian fashion. Sometimes he hit, sometimes he missed, twice he snicked it through the slips for four runs, twice he was dropped. Somehow or other, he finished the day with the stunning number of 73 not out against his name.

Now the tradition in Test cricket, of course, is that at the end of the day's play, the batting side will take a few beers into the fielding side's dressing room to have a bit of a chinwag.

Not on this day, however. Merv Hughes took in two full *eskies*. He was going to give them a blow-by-blow description of his whole innings, tell them how he felt with every run he scored and ask them how *they* were feeling as he snicked them to the fence.

Merv kept guzzling and chatting as the West Indians got in and out of the showers and towelled themselves down, and everyone was having a fine old time until suddenly . . . *szzzzzzzzzt* . . . everything fell quiet.

They looked to the door and there was the great man himself, Sir Donald Bradman, being ushered in by several South Australian cricket officials, as the ninety-year-old had expressed a desire to meet this amazing West Indian team.

And sure enough, he was introduced to them one by one as they sat along the long western wall in the visitors dressing room. As Sir Donald shuffled along, each West Indian stood up, reverentially shook his hand and had a few words so he would be able to tell his grandchildren ever afterwards about the one time he had met the great Sir Donald Bradman.

This went swimmingly until they got to the last man left on the bench, who *did not stand*. It was Patrick Patterson, six foot six inches of pure whipcord steel, the fastest fast bowler the world had ever seen. He had just got out of the showers and sat there, his towel wrapped around him, the steam rising from his rippling muscles as the whole gathering focused on what was going to happen.

Finally, Patterson stood up, towering over the diminutive five-foot-six Sir Donald, glowered down upon him and burst out with a disbelieving, 'You, Sir Donald Bradman? *You*, Sir Donald Bradman? I kill you, mon. I bowl at you, I split you in two, mon!'

Sir Donald looked up at him and without hesitation said, 'You couldn't even get f--king Merv Hughes out. You'd be no hope against me!'

———

There is a lovely postscript to this story. For on that same day, the Victorian batsman Dean Jones had also scored 103 runs and was in that same dressing room.

Now Sir Donald was rarely a loquacious man, but on this occasion he was all over Dean, telling him what a wonderful innings he'd played, how he was full of admiration for the discipline he'd shown, the way he'd played his cover drive and controlled his hook shot. Dean, of course, stood there beaming, while Merv Hughes stood on the edges waiting like a kid on Christmas morning to unwrap his own present. Because if Sir Donald was saying such things to Dean, of course he'd have to say *something* to Merv. And the big man knew that, whatever it was, he would instantly memorise it and treasure it forever more.

Finally, Sir Donald turned to go and indeed caught sight of Big Merv. He looked him up and down and then murmured to himself, 'Yeah, it's a funny game, cricket.'

# Fun, games and Gough

As part of the bid process for the Sydney Olympics—perhaps
the most crucial ingredient in Sydney's campaign—AOC president Coates hired an aircraft and pilot and criss-crossed
Africa, pressing the flesh of dignitaries of African sports asso-
ciations, Olympic committees and IOC members in return for
crucial votes. To add gravitas, Coates took Gough and Margaret
Whitlam, a master stroke, as Gough was so much admired
throughout Africa for his anti-apartheid stand.

One night they were in the back of the African beyond, dining
under the stars, when a local journalist stood up and relieved
himself only a short distance from the table. Gough didn't blink.

'Didn't that bother you, Gough?' Coates asked.

'No comrade,' the great man replied. 'Just another media leak.'

Those African votes eventually carried the day for Sydney.

# The penny drops

Steve Waugh, at a lunch at the Opera House, was asked when he knew that his career was truly over. He replied that it occurred a year or so after his retirement when he was going for a walk with his five-year-old son in the Shire, and they ran into Ricky Ponting going for a walk. The two long-time teammates chatted for a bit and then said their goodbyes.

Noting his son being a bit quiet afterwards, Steve asked him what was on his mind?

'Dad,' he said. 'How do you know Ricky Ponting?!?!'

# Wise words

The barber in Sydney's St Martin's Tower swears this is ridgy-didge.

A couple of years ago, see, the great race-horse trainer Bart Cummings comes in for a haircut just before the Spring Carnival. Has to be looking his best for the usual slew of trophies to put upon his groaning mantelpiece—likely the most over-worked bit of woodwork in the country.

Anyhoo, the barber does the usual splendid job, being very careful not to touch a single hair on those splendid eyebrows, and finally finishes, before asking—of course—Bart for a tip for the coming racing carnival.

Carefully, Bart opens his wallet, takes out a crisp lobster, a lovely new $20 note, looks him right in the eye, and says 'NEVER GAMBLE.'

# The loudest roar at origin

It was, I kid you not, a wonderfully weird, extraordinarily mesmerising moment. It was late in the first half of the State of Origin and we were 80,000 packed into Sydney's Olympic stadium.

Queensland were smashing NSW off the park and were clearly dominant, but then the Blues struck back with a wonderful Josh Morris try in the corner, from a perfectly weighted Josh Dugan kick. The stadium exploded, in a roar that went for a dinkum minute and . . .

And then those of us on the eastern side of the stands see it. It is a paper plane, thrown from high in the Gods. Even better weighted than Dugan's kick, it dips and glides, dips and glides, does a victory roll, dips and glides. There is just something about it that is so beautiful, such a *world-class* paper plane that, on our side, the roar goes up once more as everyone watches, transfixed—suddenly transported back to the schoolyards of our youth, where we could only dream of launching such a plane. Dip and glide, dip and glide . . .

It's made it over the fence! The roar goes up. It's heading towards one of the two seated security guards by the corner post on the north-eastern corner, who is watching the game, and unaware just what three-quarters of the roar behind him is about right now.

It's going to hit him! He sees it!

Reaching out from his plastic seat—a King Kong atop Empire State to the fragile frame of our plane—he grabs it and scrunches it up.

And the crowd goes wild. *Curse you, Red Baron!*

But bravo to whoever made that plane. On behalf of all of us who made paper-planes in primary school—read everyone— I say the truth:

Your achievement is the equivalent of a kid playing backyard cricket, who goes on to score a double-century at Lords.

# Intuition?

Warwick Broad was recently visiting Pisa in Italy and was dining with his girlfriend at a restaurant when a woman of Asian ethnicity approached them.

'Are you Australians?' she asked, having overheard them and noted their accents.

When they confirmed that they were, the very friendly lady asked them a few questions about the best restaurants they'd been to in Pisa etc., as she was looking for a nice place to go with friends. Then . . .

'What state are you from?' she asked.

'NSW.'

'My son used to play cricket for NSW . . .' she said, heading off into the night.

'Good night, Mrs Chee Quee,' Warwick said.

'How did you know her name?' his girlfriend asked, mystified.

# Most damaging misunderstanding

Absolutely no contest. That came in March 2001, just before the West Tigers took on the North Queensland Cowboys in Townsville. In an ante room just off the main Tiger's dressing-room, coach Terry Lamb took his block-busting winger John Hopoate aside and earnestly told him: 'Tonight Hoppa, I want you make your mark in the annals of rugby league . . .'

Hoppa, perhaps surprised at such a curious instruction, nevertheless nodded that he understood and ran out onto the field primed for the task. Alas, instead of a date with destiny, it turned out he had a destiny with dates. And the rest is history . . .

# Bad rap

Mario Fenech and his colleagues from Channel 9's *The Footy Show*, Paul Vautin and Peter Sterling, were playing golf with Sam Newman in Melbourne. At one point the others fronted Newman about the rumours that he had had a facelift.

'We had to ask him,' Fenech recounted. 'He looks like Doctor Spock. It looks like he's had Glad Wrap stretched across his face. But when we asked him, he denied it cold. He didn't blink. That's because he can't.'

# Honey Badger

For yonks, Nick Cummins, aka the Honey Badger, has been one of the most alluring characters in Australian sport—a genuine character at a time when we are not awash with them.

His more famous utterances—'I'm sweating like a gypsy with a mortgage', 'you gotta be like a midget in a urinal, you gotta be on your toes'—could get a few people offside for their lack of sensitivity, but mostly he has been celebrated for the unadulterated colour of his utterances.

Ah, sing it, Nick, after a loss suffered by his team, the Western Force: 'We were like the kid who fell out of the tree, we just weren't in it' And repeat what you said when you were named for the first time in the Wallaby squad: 'My old man woke me up in the morning. He was going off like a bag of cats.'

And when you scored your first Test try: 'I just saw the line, pinned me ears back and ended bagging a bit of meat [pie] in the corner there, which was tops!' You get the drift.

There is, however, another side of Cummins. He felt obliged to leave the Wallabies at his height to provide for his father, who had terminal prostate cancer, and his younger brother, who had terminal cystic fibrosis.

Exceptional. Nick Cummins is a national treasure and seems like a genuinely good soul.

# In the shade of Uluru

Try this for something out of the sporting dreamtime. Think Shane Gould and Evonne Goolagong-Cawley. Both have a kind of regal serenity about them; both reached great fame at much the same time, with Evonne winning her first Wimbledon championship in 1971, just before Shane won her three Olympic gold medals at the Munich Games the following year. Both are still deeply admired by their fellow Australians long after they retired.

In late 1972 a famous photo was taken of them in the pool together for a charity function, and they have kept in touch since. Early this year they were together at an Indigenous Community sports camp held beside Uluru to encourage the most talented Aboriginal sports kids from across the nation.

When each woman has said her bit to the gathering and they are relaxing with the kids, Shane notices that Evonne has racquets and balls in her car and has an idea:

'Thirty years ago you swam with me,' she says, 'and now I want to play tennis with you.'

With that, Shane traces out in the red soil the outline of a court, pokes in a few sticks to serve as the net, and they play for about twenty minutes in the shadow of the Rock, with fifty laughing Aboriginal kids chasing the balls.

No press, no nonsense. Just two great Australian sportswomen going at it as the sun beat down.

True story, told to me by Evonne!

# Colliwobbles

On ABC radio's *Grandstand*, presenter Karen Tighe asked listeners to name their dream final for the Rugby World Cup. The first caller was from Adelaide, the conversation going something like this:

Tighe: 'I hope Australia is one of your teams.'
Caller: 'Yes.'
Tighe: 'And who do you hope will be their opponents?'
Caller: 'Collingwood.'
Tighe: 'Collingwood! Why Collingwood?!'
Caller. 'I want to see them get flogged again.'

# The 'egoless' Australians

The following is brought to you straight from *The Wall Street Journal*, as the opening paragraphs of a feature piece in June 2015.

'The safest way to win an NBA championship is to land one of the league's few unstoppable players. This is the superstar theory of basketball, and the Golden State Warriors and Cleveland Cavaliers are proof that it's as powerful as ever. They're in the NBA Finals this week because they happen to be the teams with Stephen Curry and LeBron James.

'But even superstars require the right surrounding parts, and both the Warriors and Cavaliers have one player who isn't an obvious reason for their run to the Finals—except to the few people who know why they are important.

'They are the Australians. And every team in the NBA could use one.

'It seems like a strange coincidence that Golden State center Andrew Bogut and Cleveland guard Matthew Dellavedova are Australians playing the same supporting roles in this year's Finals that San Antonio Spurs forward Patty Mills mastered last season and Luc Longley pioneered on the championship Chicago Bulls teams of the 1990s.

'But what if it isn't?

'The few Americans who actually know Australian basketball say they're not at all surprised that Dellavedova and

Bogut have emerged as indispensable pieces in the play-offs. Australian players, they say, tend to be the opposites of most American players. They don't seek superstardom. They actively avoid attention. They excel in the egoless roles that most players reject.'

And there you go. If you were wondering why Greg Norman never took up basketball, I think you have your answer.

# IT WAS BETTER IN MY DAY

Why Stirling Moss was never World Champion perhaps

'Alfie [Langer] could fill a rubbish bin full of spew in the sheds before kick-off.'
Trevor Gillmeister, reminiscing fondly in *Rugby League Week*.

'Stretching. Lonhro won a lot of races and you never saw him stretching his foreleg on the fence before running.'
The redoubtable Tommy Raudonikis, responding to a question as to why so many players suffered hamstring strains these days.

'I've seen how football has gone, from blokes with beards to now a heap of pretty boys running around. It's quite a contrast.'
Brad Fittler, after playing his 300th first-grade game. Ain't that the truth.

'Formula One's not a sport, it's a business now. If Lewis Hamilton wins a race he has to go speak to Vodafone. If I won, I'd try and chase a bit of crumpet.'
The 82-year-old motor racing legend Sir Stirling Moss, reminisces, in the pages of the mighty *Guardian*.

'Well, for one thing, I've noticed the current generation of Wallabies are not having as much fun as we used to.'
John Eales when asked how it felt to be retired, just a week after the event.

*'My head has taken more hits than Google.'*
Barry Michael, 57, former Australian boxing champion, at a lunch on the Gold Coast.


*'A mate of mine has wanted to come to the Hong Kong Sevens for years. He's finally convinced his wife. But he has to take her shopping in the swish Stanley Market afterwards, and also shopping up to Beijing for a week. In the old days, you were a good guy if you lifted your feet when she was vacuuming . . .'*
Former All Blacks winger and New Zealand Sevens captain, Eric Rush.

# Lithgow flashback

There was a light at the end of the tunnel. And noise, a solid sonic boom that simply didn't stop. Marjorie Jackson walked tremulously to her fate. Around her, others of her ilk were taking steps with equal trepidation. There was no way out, no way back. Men in uniform walked at their side.

This was it, the final of the women's 100 metres at the 1952 Helsinki Olympics.

Out of the tunnel, and into the stadium proper. 'Our Marj', our very own, very shy Marj, from Lithgow, couldn't stop shaking. Looking around at the vast, roaring stadium of 100,000 people, she was simply staggered that she and the other seven women could be at the centre of all this attention. 'I'd never seen anywhere that number of people in my life and I remember thinking to myself, "What on Earth am I doing here?"' Jackson told me, in late 2004.

Lithgow, a coalmining town about 100 kilometres to the west of the Sydney Harbour Bridge, was a great place to grow up. Marj Jackson was the middle of three daughters of a worker at the local munitions factory and his wife. For Marj, school was fun, sport was fun, running fast was fun. But neither she nor the hordes she left in her wake could help noticing that she actually won all of the school races she was in with ridiculous ease, despite her rather ungraceful way of running.

Although her school chums nicknamed her 'Bernborough', after the famous racehorse of the day, at full flight the young

Marjorie Jackson was as ungainly as a baby giraffe at full stretch—all arm and legs thrashing around without seeming rhyme, rhythm or reason—and, despite her speed, it was obvious she wasn't getting the best out of herself.

'Dad thought I could use some help so he got a man who worked with him in the factory, by the name of Jim Monaghan, to start to teach me,' she said. So it was that Monaghan, a former sprinter of note, set about changing what Marj's dad was pleased to call her 'style'.

Young 'Bernborough' was soon winning with even more ridiculous ease than before. It was time to take on some stiffer competition. She wasn't long in arriving. 'In 1949, the Australian athletic officials invited Fanny Blankers-Koen, the winner of four gold sprinting medals at the London Olympics, to Australia,' Jackson recounted. 'It was sort of a promotional thing to have her race here, as she was also the world-record holder in the 100m.' With a lot of other equally anonymous local talent, Marjorie was invited to come down to the Sydney Sports Ground to run against the famous Dutch flyer.

'I was very nervous,' she said, 'and started vomiting all over the place before we got to the starting line.' Unfortunately for the Dutchwoman, that didn't slow Marj any, and the unknown lass from Lithgow smoked her and the rest of the field. Beat her by three yards, going away, and then did the same in another race a week later to prove she wasn't just a Lithgow flash in the pan.

'I was quite stunned that I beat her,' Jackson told me. 'And also very pleased.'

Careful though. Not too pleased. There was to be none of this getting too big a head about things. 'I'll never forget Dad saying to me, after I'd been flouncing around a bit: "If you're going to keep on running, I've got one thing to say to you and one thing only. God has given everyone a gift and it just so happens that yours is running and you mustn't think you're better than anyone else because of it".'

She confirmed her extraordinary talent by winning three gold medals at Auckland's Empire Games the very next year, in the 100-yards, 220-yards and the 440-yards relay. Her athletics career had been well and truly launched, and pretty soon it seemed all of Australia was talking about the 'Lithgow Flash'.

'The rest of my life didn't change, though,' she said. 'Athletics was strictly amateur in those days, so I was broke all the time—I stayed living at home, and kept working as a typist in a local co-op.'

Inevitably, the focus of the locals fell on the coming Helsinki Olympic Games, and just what chances our Marj would have of bringing home a gold medal. One obvious problem was that, while the local lass was used to running only on grass, the track at Helsinki was going to be cinders, a material almost as hard as concrete.

Something had to be done, and it was. As it was well before large dollops of money could be garnered from the Institute for Great and Public Glory in faraway Canberra, it was left to the Lithgow community to overcome the problem and organise a decent training track for her. Lamingtons. They were the answer. They were baked in the homes and sold on the street. And chook raffles—in every pub around for miles.

The materials were bought, and with the help of that other great Australian institution—the good old Saturday morning working bee—the track was built under the supervision of the local council. 'There wasn't enough money left over to build lights, so every night after I finished work I had to train by the headlights of Mr Monaghan's car,' Jackson said.

Flying to Helsinki with the rest of the Olympic team, something significant happened to Marjorie Jackson. 'We were all sitting there quietly, no-one knew anyone else—and in those days you didn't speak to anybody else unless you'd been first introduced—when the boxing manager stood up and said "This is ridiculous, we're going away for two months as a team, and no-one is speaking to each other",' Jackson said. 'So he made us all move around the plane and mingle and introduce ourselves and this fellow came up to me and said he was a cyclist and his name was Peter Nelson.'

A lithe and lively fellow, he seemed to be looking rather warmly at her for some reason. Matter of fact, Marj Jackson rather liked the cut of his jib, too.

And now, here she was. At last, at the starting line of the Olympic 100 metres final. There was still no way out, nothing else to do but knuckle down and run.

Back home in Lithgow, she knew, it was 3 am, and her parents were sitting in their living room with most of the neighbourhood and three short-wave radios trying to pick up the faint and faraway signal.

She put her blocks down at the start—the same wooden ones her dad had made for her in his backyard shed—and made ready to rumble.

*Ready . . .*

'I was still nervous, and shaking as I put my fingers on the starting line,' Jackson said. 'But I kept saying to myself, "I'm as good as they are until they prove otherwise".'

*Set . . .*

'I was really conscious that I didn't want to jump the gun in my nervousness.'

**GO LIKE THE CLAPPERS!**

126

'I just ran. I forgot all my nervousness and just ran. I focused on the white tape and ran towards it as fast as my legs could carry me.'

Which was pretty fast—certainly faster than anyone else—and she breasted the tape a good 5 metres ahead of her nearest rival in the world-record-equalling time of 11.5 seconds.

After the race, and as the first Australian woman to win an Olympic track and field gold medal, she turned to the athletes' section of the stand where the Australians were sitting. Peter Nelson was there, waving his flag nineteen to the dozen, obviously beaming with pride and maybe something else besides.

'I don't think I've been more emotional than when they put up the Australian flag and played the national anthem,' she recalled. 'It was a moment in time that was mine and it can never be taken away from me. Whatever happens, I hope I don't ever get Alzheimer's disease, because I don't ever want to forget it. Ever.'

At the Helsinki Games she also won the 200 metres and at the 1954 Vancouver Empire Games, she won another three gold medals. Within a year of returning home from Helsinki, she had married Peter Nelson and settled in a town just out of Adelaide, where they opened a sports store together. After Vancouver, she announced her retirement and no amount of pleading from the public, the press or officials could change her mind.

'It was the right decision,' she said. 'When I do anything in my life, I like to commit myself to it 100 per cent or not at all. I had been committed like that to athletics and now it was my marriage. I always knew that athletics was something just for a short time, while my marriage was forever.'

Unfortunately her husband was not. 'After 24 years of wonderful married life together,' she recalled softly, 'and raising our three children, he suddenly fell ill. The doctors said it was leukaemia. He said he would beat it, and I thought he would, but in the end it was obvious he wasn't going to. He asked me to bring him home so he could die. I nursed him until he did. I lost him only ten days after he came home.'

Much of Marjorie Nelson's energy since then has been spent in raising money for the Peter Nelson Leukaemia Foundation, which funds research into the illness. She remained involved with athletics and was the general manager of the 1994 Commonwealth Games team. She served as State Governor of South Australia from 2001–07; in 2007 she was given the Olympic Order, the highest order bestowed by the IOC. Its citation stated that the award was made for her 'having illustrated the Olympic ideal through her actions, having achieved remarkable merit in the sporting world and having rendered outstanding service to the Olympic movement through her community work and as Governor of South Australia'.

So that's the Lithgow Flash. A fine woman, a strong presence, a great Australian.

# One of a kind, long gone

Steve Merrick arrived out of a clear blue sky when Bob Dwyer picked him fresh from the Singleton coalmines to replace George Gregan as Wallaby halfback in 1995. He played wonderfully well against the All Blacks, while all around him rugby was in total turmoil as the Kerry Packer-backed World Rugby Corporation and the Rupert Murdoch-backed Australian Rugby Union fought like two cats in a sack for control of the game.

Despite being offered several hundred thousand dollars to sign with one or the other, Merrick declined. For starters, he didn't want to live in Sydney.

'I couldn't live here,' he said flatly. 'I want to live in a place where you can play cricket in the street and get twenty overs in before the first car comes.' And nor was he interested in any of these million-dollar contracts they were bandying around. 'I don't really want to think about it,' he told me at the time. 'What is important to me is not losing my trade union ticket. That's where real financial security for me and my missus comes from and, whatever happens, I don't want to lose that.'

On ya, Steve. You were one of a kind, and you did the old game proud.

# Newk

Three-time Wimbledon winner, John Newcombe, once told me the story of when he was 18 years old and had just lost an important junior tournament to Tony Roche after having been out partying till 3 am the previous night. That evening, his father, an amiable and caring type of fellow, an accountant up Lane Cove way, decided it was time to have a quiet word with his son around the family dinner table.

'Son,' he said, 'you can either be a great athlete or a great playboy . . . but you can't be both. You're going to have to choose one or the other.'

In response Newcombe the Younger looks his father right in the eyes and gives his reply: 'I'll tell you what, Dad, I'm going to give *both* of them a heck of a shot.'

# The 2015 NRL Grand Final was great, but not the greatest

The 2015 rugby league grand final? Loved it. Was there. A dramatic extra-time Johnathan Thurston field goal seals a fairy-tale NRL grand final victory for the North Queensland Cowboys over the Brisbane Broncos.

But, no, you young'uns, it was not the best-ever grand final.

The rest of us, who are older, wiser, and have seen a thing or two, know the truth. We know that though the 2015 Grand Final was fantastic, and the 1997 Grand Final ran it close, there remains just one grand final—in the red corner—that is still the heavyweight champeen of all grand finals . . . and that is the 1989 Grand Final! Oh you whipper-snappers, you young 'uns, you littlies, you shoulda been there! We were.

Balmain Tigers v Canberra Raiders. At the Sydney Football Stadium. Beautiful September day. This was sporting theatre like they just don't make it any more. There were so many characters that were all just a little larger than life, characters we all knew, and are still revered to this day: Mal Meninga, Bradley Clyde, Ricky Stuart, John 'Chicka' Ferguson, Laurie Daley were standouts for the Raiders, while Balmain boasted the likes of Garry Jack, Paul Sironen, Benny Elias, Wayne Pearce, Steve 'Blocker' Roach, all with the redoubtable Warren Ryan as coach.

With just 15 minutes to go and the Tigers holding onto a 12-8 lead, Warren Ryan decides to replace his big prop, Roach, with a faster, fresher, defender. Roach doesn't want to go but has no choice, and leaves the field grumbling fiercely. (Something that has continued for the next 26 years, seeing as you ask, but I digress.)

A penalty to the Tigers to make it 14-8 puts the Tigers in a strong position, but still the Raiders keep doing exactly that—launching raid, after raid, after raid. As the minutes ebb away and the seconds tick down, everyone has one eye on the field and one eye on the clock. The Raiders are throwing EVERYTHING at them. Can the Tigers hold on?

Amazingly, Elias is twice able to move himself into position to make field-goal attempts—either one of which would have sealed the deal—but both just miss. (One bounced back from the cross-bar.)

The Raiders . . . They're still going! And now, look there!

With just 90 seconds to go, the Raiders' kick goes up—a swirling up-and-under—and a slew of Raiders and Tigers go up for it. It comes down the Raiders' side. Daley has it! He hoicks it into the arms of Ferguson, on the fly. Chicka says he's 35 years old, but others reckon he's older than religion. Who cares?

He jinks, he jives, he jinks three more times and scores the try! With a conversion by Meninga, it is all locked up, 14-14, and extra time is upon us. With just three minutes of that extra time left, it happens. Out on the right wing is the most unheard-of footballer we'd never heard of, Steve Jackson! No. 20 on his back, a 23-year-old reserve who has just come off the bench. We've never seen him before. We've never seen him since.

But this, this is his moment. He's got the ball, 25 metres out! He shimmies! He shakes! He bumps off one of the Tigers! Two of the Tigers! THREE of them. He twirls, somehow, without really slowing down . . . even as three Tigers close in on him.

They nail him just before the line, hitting him as one. But that bastard is still going!

He reaches out his right hand, and plonks it down for the biscuits, the victory, the 1989 premiership!

Still the most stunning and exciting try I've ever seen. The incarnation of the try of our dreams, the one we imagined as kids we might one day score, but never did. Meninga cries tears of joy. Pearce, tears of anguish.

Yes, I repeat, the 2015 Grand Final was fabulous, but the 1989 vintage is still the Grange Hermitage of the collection. We old-timers get that.

Pass me my pipe, and I'll tell you about it again.

# Simple

Before a Test against the All Blacks 25 years ago, Bob Dwyer talked to us for 45 minutes about how he wanted us to play, most particularly the back line. I really concentrated, but could only get 5 per cent, at best, of what he was on about. Afterwards, I asked my captain, Nick Farr-Jones, if he understood.

'Ninety eight per cent of it,' Nick said broadly, 'was run straight, draw your man, and set up the bloke outside you.'

BINGO! The essence of it was simple and the rest was just needless complications. I got it.

Then, ten years ago at a rugby lunch in Perth, a Super 12 coach was holding forth on the art of coaching by statistics, on how it was done in the modern day, courtesy of statisticians, computers, and endless analysis of the games his own team had played, and those played by their forthcoming opponents.

'For we have done the work,' I recall him saying, as part of a general theme. 'And we now understand that on average, Richie McCaw will touch the ball 67.234 times in a match, and if we don't get him below 59.892 times, we won't win the match. Same with turnovers. The Crusaders on average have 9.543 turnovers in a match, and they never lose a match when their turnovers are below 6.423, while our turnovers are now at 10.436 and we've never won a match when it is higher than 14.304 times and . . .'

And so on.

He sat down, to a rather stunned silence that was quickly filled by the MC, Ray Seger, who brought the house down when he said: 'I don't know if that was a rugby speech, or a f--king BINGO call!'

Such memories confirm my strongly-held belief that sport was never actually meant to be that complicated, and that those who pretend it is rocket surgery risk losing their way, just as coaches who succumb to it risk having their teams lose their way.

Which brings me to Eddie Jones, more recently, speaking at a breakfast put on by the Hunters Hill Rugby Club. To the England coach's eternal credit—and demonstrating his commitment to the grass-roots of the game—despite being rugby's Messiah of the Moment, Eddie took the stage to be interviewed by Gordon Bray, just as he had agreed to do three months previously, before he turned into that Messiah.

And it was spell-binding.

No gibberish.

No statistics.

No talk of red-zones, green-zones, black-zones. No gibberish about channels. No percentage plays.

He talked mostly about the importance of picking players with the right character and then working them harder than the teams they were playing against.

Statistics?

I am paraphrasing, because I wasn't taking notes like a grown-up journo, but broadly what he said was this, and the last two sentences are exact quotes: 'You can make statistics do anything you like, and some coaches really believe in them, but I don't. There are only two statistics we look at. Firstly, how long does it take a player to get up off the ground and get back in his place for defence. Secondly, how long it takes a player to get up off the ground and get back in his place for attack.'

BINGO!

Here was the Messiah of the Moment—and no doubt for some years to come—saying that when it all boiled down, the game really isn't that complicated, and if you get the basics right, and fill it with fit blokes who really want to have a go, the rest will take care of itself!

Music to my cauliflower ears.

# Vale Jack Taylor

England's legendary football referee, Jack Taylor, who died at the age of 82, among other things presided over the 1974 World Cup final. But the best story about him goes back to the time he was hit by a flying penny thrown by a Luton fan, after the home side had lost a match at Kenilworth Road, leaving a gash that had to be stitched.

To settle it all down, Luton Club's most famous director, Eric Morecambe—of Morecambe & Wise fame—visited Taylor to apologise.

'And, umm, you won't report us, will you?' the funny man asked anxiously.

'No,' Taylor replied, generously.

'Good,' says Morecambe. 'Now can I have my penny back?'

# A bad call

And now let's cross down to the sideline for Darryl Brohman to give his report during a Waratahs v Brumbies match some many years ago:

'Both referees are having bad games. Mr Turner's having a shocker and George Gregan isn't doing much better!'

# Cadle rocked

Back in 2000, a nice knockabout sports journo by the name of John Gilmour is at the finish line calling over the loudspeaker the final stages of the Hornsby to Swansea Cycling Classic. And as this scrawny kid crosses the line in 19th position, he says: 'And ladies and gentlemen, please put your hands together for . . .' (*strange name, not sure how to pronounce it, but it probably rhymes with cradle*) '. . . Cadle Evans.'

A short time later Gilmour, standing on a platform, looks down to see said rider glaring up at him, wanting a word. Yes, kid?

'My name,' the young fellow says pointedly, 'is Cadel, like Ka-dell, not Cadle.'

Gilmour has seen uppity smart-aleck kids like this before. 'Listen,' he says, covering the microphone so no one can hear. 'No one gives a f--k. This is the Swansea Classic—no one cares. Who do you think you are? The Tour de France winner?'

# The day Midget Farrelly surfed
## the perfect wave

Midget Farrelly, who passed away in August 2016, aged 71, was one of most likeable, charismatic Australian sportsmen I've ever met.

I once asked him if, in his whole career, one particular wave stood out as the perfect wave. His response was both eloquent and heart-felt.

The background to it is that in 1962 Farrelly was the first non-Hawaiian to win a surfing contest at Makaha Beach, on the western side of the splendid isle of Oahu. In 1968 the iconic Australian surfing champion was there again, perchance on the day when the biggest surf ever recorded in those parts was pounding in.

And then, pushing four decades later—and by then fairly anonymous in this part of the world—Midget happened to be passing through Hawaii with his wife of four decades, Bev, and decided to go back for a look.

Things had changed.

While the beach and surf were as pristine and magical as ever, the beachfront suburb was going through notably tough times, with something of a menacing drug culture having taken over. So it was that while Bev stayed in the locked car, Midget took his board out.

Way out.

Somehow, the further out you got, the more pure it became—Hawaii, as it always was, and always would be, without the corrosive influences of other worlds descending upon it.

In the gathering dusk, just one other surfer was there, a large native Hawaiian of mature years. Such is the protocol of such things that the Australian from Sydney's northern beaches, a visitor to these shores, kept his distance.

But the other surfer soon paddled over. 'Hey, Midget . . .' he said, by way of greeting, in his thick Hawaiian accent.

The bloke remembered him, and they talked of times past. Of that win in 1962; of that day in 1968 with that shattering surf, when the legendary Greg Noll had ridden his last big wave; of what had happened in Makaha since.

This, Midget was thinking, this is the real Hawaii experience, not the stuff on the shore.

'Hey Midget,' the man spoke again as a big wave loomed, and he moved his own board well out of the way, 'you take this wave.'

It was classic, classic Hawaiian culture, where giving what you have is always the first order of things.

Midget Farrelly thanked him and farewelled him, even as the swell rose to a roaring beauty and, as just one with the setting sun, he was once again scything and twirling his way back to Bev, up and down the face of a surviving bit of nature's nirvana.

'And that,' he told me, 'that was the perfect wave.'

# Off in a puff: why Reg Gasnier was one of the greats

Reg Gasnier was from a time when sport was more Camelot than Corporate.

Born close enough to Jubilee Oval that he took the crowd's roar with his mother's milk, he was like all the boys at Mortdale Primary, in that he had only one dream—to play for the mighty Dragons.

But there was a key difference between Reggie and the others. He demonstrated extraordinary talent from the first, and they didn't.

See, it just so happened that his natural game was *the* game, the one others would try to emulate, without ever quite getting there. He had speed, he had swerve, he had verve, he had an acceleration that would leave others standing, and a particular capacity to pull off massive side-steps without losing pace.

He scored so many tries as a schoolboy that in 1957 the Dragons asked Reg to play grade, even though he was still only 17—something that he was *desperate* to do. 'Not on your Nelly,' said Reg's dad, and not even the next year when the Dragons were *begging*. Young Reg in his view was not ready for it yet and needed to continue develop his natural game, unstomped upon by full grown men.

In 1959 though, Dad Gasnier allowed Reg to play and it all came together. Gasnier had graduated to playing reserve grade, and when the centre in Firsts hurt his leg at training, Reg got the call. Get your boots laced, son, you're on.

And off and running. And swerving, and accelerating and decelerating, stepping off both feet, and picking gaps that others didn't even know were there. So began for Gasnier the season to end reason. From a standing start in reserve grade, he became a regular first grader, and then made the NSW team!

Not that he was allowed to get a big head. Down St George way it was always the club first and, after returning from rep training with NSW, the Saints coach, 'Killer' Kearney, would growl, 'You're with St George now, get your head out of the clouds . . . Don't get carried away with yourself, son, you're part of a *team*.'

And not just any team, dammit, but the ST GEORGE team.

A Saints team, in fact, that won the grand final that year, as it did every year in that era. That night, Gasnier was picked for his first Kangaroo tour. Praise the Lord, and pass me a jersey. A Kangaroo jersey.

Though he was really just taken along for experience more than anything else, Gasnier was so outstanding in the lead-up games he was selected for the first Test, where he scored three tries in a famous Australian victory. England came back to win the second Test by a sole point, setting up a classic showdown in the final Test, where he played a key role in a try that was hailed in both the English and Australian press as 'one of the greatest tries ever scored'.

After retiring eight years later with 36 more Tests to his credit, he was highly regarded enough in the game to become one of the four initial 'Immortals'.

# Reg Gasnier: a role model before his time

I received an interesting reminiscence about Reg Gasnier from reader Paul Kilroy, about how, as a 12-year-old visiting Sydney from Grafton in 1964, his dad took him to St George training at Jubilee Oval on the Thursday night where he could see all of his heroes at once. Norm Provan! Johnny Raper! Graeme Langlands! Reg Gasnier! Billy Smith, Kevin Ryan, Poppa Clay, Dick Huddart, and Ian Walsh! As the players wandered onto the field, his dad approached a few and asked would they mind saying a couple of words to his son.

Johnny Raper obliged, but it was Gasnier who stood out. 'He warmly and respectfully shook my father's and my hand, and engaged us enthusiastically. He said to stick around and, when training was finished, he'd take us into the sheds and introduce us around. True to his word, he did just that. I got to shake all their hands and came away in a state of absolute euphoria. As a young league fan from the bush, I felt like I was floating on air for months to come.'

And the feeling never quite left him. 'This event had a lifelong effect on me. It taught me many things. I have thought about it often in the ensuing years and came to a realisation that it was not Gasnier's sporting prowess or ego at play that night but his humanity, his decency and his sense of responsibility to rugby league. He was a man who transcended mere sport. And this in an era when the term "role model" was not in the English language.'

# A few good props

Back in 1978, the Wallabies were about to play the All Blacks at Eden Park. On the morning of the match, stand-in manager Ross Turnbull talked to the team and then asked the backs to leave him with the forwards. The door shut, and it was just Turnbull with the pigs.

'Look,' he said, waving an airy hand at the just-departed backs, 'these Phantom comic swappers and Mintie eaters, these blond-headed fly-weights are one thing, and we will need them after the hard work's done. But the real stuff's got to be done right here by you blokes.'

The Wallabies went on to a famous win, and that story, recounted by one of the forwards in the room, Chris Handy, has always been the best exposition of the difference between backs and forwards.

# Miller-lite

It was not the green, green grass of home, and yet ... it was greener still.

It was the green of Lords cricket oval, just two weeks after the Second World War was over. May, of 1945. And this was the first of the famed Victory Tests, which were to be five encounters between the finest flannelled men that the armed services of England and Australia could throw at each other.

Sitting in the players' pavilion, the dashing Australian pilot, Flying Officer Keith Miller, was enjoying the sunshine and watching as one of his own, with bat in hand, slowly made his way out of the pavilion and onto the ground proper to take his spot at the crease.

His name was Graham Williams, a former South Australian Sheffield Shield player who'd been shot down in the Middle East five years earlier, and spent the rest of the war in a German POW camp. Just two weeks earlier, he'd been liberated; and, though he'd lost an extraordinary amount of weight, an article had appeared in *The Times* that very morning, detailing his story and announcing that he would play.

Even fifty years later, the memory of what happened that morning would be enough to make Miller mist over with emotion, with his voice—that of an old man now—quavering as he tried to get through the story without breaking down.

'So he started to walk out. I can see him now, his back straight, looking all around at Lord's—it was made to hold 28,000 but there were 30,000 there that day. Lots were sitting on the grass. Naturally, as he walked out, people began to whisper to each other, *P-O-W, shot down . . . released two weeks ago . . .* and that sort of thing.

'And as he walked out, everyone quietly stood and started this *clap . . . clap . . . clap*.

'Now I have heard people clapping at Lord's many times. I've heard applause for wonderful batting and bowling from great players. But this was applause with a difference. It was muffled and ongoing. As he walked, everybody stayed standing and continued this beautiful, hushed applause.

'And I can see him walking out there, his head going from side to side, looking around him, saying, *Where am I? Can this be true?* Poor feller had lost quite a bit of weight.'

It was the moment Miller remembered perhaps best from that whole time, on the cusp as it was between his war days and his even more legendary days wearing the baggy green cap of Australia.

It's hard to guess the effect the war might have had on Miller's subsequent approach to cricket. But he was once asked why he never seemed to get too excited upon the taking of a crucial wicket, and his reply perhaps gives a clue to his thinking: 'I guess you don't do those sort of things when you've known what it's like to have a Messerschmitt up your arse.'

# Alan McGilvray

When I was growing up, as the youngest of seven children on our farm at Peats Ridge, the great ABC cricket broadcaster Alan McGilvray was the sound of our summers.

Dad always had with him a battered trannie, held together with wire, insulating tape and prayer. So we might be picking away in one row of tomatoes when Dad's head would pop up from another row with the news that 'Lillee's got another one!' and we would all take a merciful break from picking for a while to gather round Dad for the details.

During a good Ashes series, like when Dennis Lillee and Jeff Thomson were terrorising the Pommies in 1975, we sometimes seemed to do more listening to cricket than picking tomatoes, but Dad never minded. For, you see, the working days passed easily when Mr McGilvray was on the trannie.

What a pleasure and an honour it was, thus, some three decades later, to interview Mr McGilvray in his home in Double Bay, not long before he passed away. By then, he was an old man, and I was ushered into the presence of an obviously frail and distinguished white-haired gentleman, sitting in an old, brown lounge-chair, looking out at the garden.

'I'm sorry I can't get up,' he says in much the same mellifluous voice that used to roll across Australia for nigh on 50 summers. 'I'm not well.'

That much, too, was obvious, as he sat midst a walking frame and various other medical paraphernalia, still in his pyjamas, though it is late morning. The friendly garden lizard that has come in from under the door to crawl up the lounge-chair and on to his right arm is not brushed away.

'I've had a couple of strokes in just the last six months,' recounted Mr McGilvray, 'and before that a very bad fall which gave me multiple fractures of my hips and pelvis, so things have been difficult.'

In a reflective mood, looking back over his long life, Mr McGilvray took me to a time sixty years earlier. It was in Sydney Town, in December 1933.

The young Alan McGilvray, formerly of Sydney Grammar, and now working hard in his father's footwear factory, was on a night out with his fiancée, Gwen, at the Regent Theatre. Suddenly a message flashed up on the screen: *Would Mr Alan McGilvray report to the manager's office, please.* With no little trepidation— had something gone wrong at home?—McGilvray excused himself from his fiancée.

It was his father on the phone, telling him that he had been selected to make his debut in the NSW Sheffield Shield side on its coming tour to Victoria and South Australia.

Out on the No. 1 platform on Sydney's Central Station a few days later, Gwen was there again, with all his family and a lot of his friends—all gathered to see him off. There was the usual round of handshakes, kisses, fare-thee-wells and back-slapping, all of which his father viewed from a small distance.

Then, when the time was right and the train was giving its first serious hisses to show it was making ready to leave, Mr McGilvray Snr took Alan a little away from the well-wishers for a quiet word. 'Son,' he said, 'I don't know where this game is taking you or what it's going to do to you, but I want you to promise me one thing . . . that you'll leave this game better for having been a part of it.'

Moved at the memory, Mr McGilvray pauses a moment, and then continues, with wonder now in his voice. 'And do you know whom I saw in that first compartment?' he asks rhetorically. 'Just in that first one there were Alan Kippax, Don Bradman, Tiger O'Reilly and Stan McCabe.'

It was indeed a special kind of team that young McGilvray had broken into, full of world cricketing talent, and he was under no illusion as to his very lowly position in the illustrious pecking order.

His first touch of serious Shield action was to come several days later at the Melbourne Cricket Ground, just before Christmas. He was to bat at No. 5 and Kippax, the NSW captain, gave him just one instruction: 'I want you to hang around there with Bradman, let him get the runs,' he growled, 'and I want you to bat the whole session through, whatever happens.'

And that was that.

'So I walked out with the great man,' Mr McGilvray recalled. As they proceeded to the pitch together—the unknown debutant and the legend who had rewritten the record books—the younger man couldn't help but notice that all 50,000 at the ground seemed to be on their feet and roaring.

Something got into the young fellow. Nervous as hell, but feeling that he simply had to say something to show the occasion had not got the better of him, he turned to the senior man and said: 'Fancy that, Braddles, isn't it nice how all these people have come out just to see me bat.' (He could at least call him 'Braddles' because the two had known each other for some time through club cricket.)

In reply, the great man said not a word, made not a gesture, but merely looked back at him with what McGilvray later described as 'an odd kind of look that I will never forget as long as I live', and walked on to the crease.

Our Don Bradman did well, on his way to an eventual 187 not out, while McGilvray also kept his end up, scoring 11 on his own account, though falling on the last ball before lunch to 'a ball from Fleetwood-Smith which cut inside me and took my off-stump'.

And no, he did not go on to a brilliant representative cricketing career himself, managing to play just twenty matches for NSW, at an average of 24 runs per innings, but, no matter. Fate had other great things in store, and it first came knocking a couple of years later.

'At the end of a day's play against Queensland at the Gabba, this chap came up and said would I mind saying a few words on ABC Radio about it, and I said "not at all".'

Whatever McGilvray might have lacked in raw cricketing ability, he made up for in intuitive understanding of the game and the players, and he did well enough in that first stint of radio to be invited back again. And, as it turned out, again and again and again. He went on to call 219 Tests, going all the way to 1985, 'when I'd simply had enough'.

When I interviewed him, ten years later, he felt exactly the same way about life.

'No, I've had enough. I've had a wonderful life, known wonderful people, but it will be a relief to me to go. I am crippled, I can't move. I don't want to go on. I miss my wife terribly, my children all live far away though they do what they can, as do my grandchildren. But I . . . have had . . . enough.'

The emotion with which he said this was underlined by his deliberate action of directing his voice right at my tape-recorder sitting on the armchair rest beside him—to make sure I and anyone else who reads this is getting the message—and by the single tear that rolled all the way down his right cheek.

It was the most moved I have ever been by an interview. One way or another though, he had kept his promise to his father.

# Alf on the ball

This was an exchange between referee Bill Harrigan and Broncos captain Allan Langer in the late nineties.

Langer, you'll recall, had a reputation for giving a bit of lip and was always questioning the referee whenever a penalty was given, with comments such as 'What's that for?' and 'They've been doing it all day and you haven't penalised them.'

In this particular game, the penalty count was 5-1 against the Broncos, and 'Alfie' was on his usual behaviour. So, when Harrigan blew another penalty against the Broncos, Alfie made a beeline to him to remonstrate.

Seeing Alfie on his way, Bill waved his arm and said, 'Go away, Alfie, go away. Just go away . . .'

To which Alfie cheekily replied, 'Is that an instruction or a request?'

To regain some sense of authority, Bill sternly responded with, 'What's the difference?'

Knowing the ref was expecting him to simply to walk away, Alfie hesitated for a moment before replying with, 'I don't do requests!'

# Kerry O

The following is an excerpt from an interview *Inside Sport* did with the great Kerry O'Keeffe.

O'Keeffe: 'I coached a junior camp with Merv Hughes once. We got on the bus and there are about 60 11-year-olds. Merv was last on. And there he was, this moustachioed brute of a fast bowler with cred. "Morning boys!" he said. "Morning Mr Hughes," they nervously replied. Then Merv goes: "Hang on . . ." before cocking his leg and letting rip with this blood-curdler. [Laugh.] Kids were diving everywhere. That's when I knew that the modern player didn't have the airs and graces of the former player.'

How was cricket camp?
Merv Hughes taught us how to fart really loud.

# Wisdom on cue

I met Eddie Charlton in 1993. He was then 64 and it was hard to believe he had ever been anything other than the smooth, carefully coiffured, minutely manicured fellow coming out of the lift at the Sydney Tattersalls Club to greet me.

'Hello, pleased to meet you,' says the man himself, as he changes the snooker cue from his right to his left hand, and proffers a handshake.

And pleased to meet you Mr Charlton. But the thought remains. Polished shoes, pleated trousers, double-breaster, after-shave—this guy's got the works.

As a matter of fact though, there was a time when things were a whole lot different . . .

Imagine, if you can, little Eddie at all of nine years old, shifting around the billiard table with his bare feet the soft-drink crate he needs to stand on. He's in his grandfather's pool hall up Swansea way, south of Newcastle, and the only way he can get his hands properly above the table is to keep moving the crate around for every shot.

A hiss from the front door: 'Ediieee! Sergeant Toby's coming along the street!'

As always, Eddie would drop to his knees and scurry under the table, even as the fishermen and miners who were the regulars would quickly gather round that particular table to shield him from view.

Then, through the forest of legs, Eddie would catch the barest glimpse of the kindly Sergeant Toby poking his head in the door, quickly looking around to make sure that young Eddie wasn't hanging around again. Then he would withdraw, satisfied, and it was back to business. Black ball in the corner pocket. Seven points to the bare-foot kid.

Eddie loved playing snooker. From the first time his grandfather had showed him how to play, when Eddie was about eight years old, it had just gripped him. He began to practise before school, sometimes during lunch hours, after school.

He loved it so much he ended up pretty much moving from his parents' house and in with his grandparents, behind the pool hall, so he'd have more time to practise and play. His parents understood, and certainly did not share the attitude of many of Eddie's schoolfriends' parents, that all such places were 'dens of iniquity'.

And Eddie was good, no doubt about that. Cleaned 'em all up—all the regulars and all their mates, and not a few of their mates' mates at that. Bit by bit it became obvious to grandfather Joe that he had a bit of a prodigy on his hands.

Eddie. Eddie. Eddie. The name began to reverberate in the region as all and sundry wanted to play him or see him play.

Mr Charlton, you tell it: 'So then my grandfather would pack me into the car with the cues, and we'd start travelling all over the place, up and down the coast and inland, taking on whoever wanted to play.'

Cessnock, Maitland, Newcastle, Kurri Kurri. On and on. They all fell to Eddie's cue.

There was, of course, betting—heavy betting. The mines were all at full tilt, everyone was employed, all had money in their pocket. And on all of their road trips, and a lot of the games at

Yellow Green
Red Blue
Brown Pink
Black

R e g

the Swansea billiard rooms beside, grandfather Joe would run a book, always backing with his own money little Eddie to win.

It meant that Eddie learnt about pressure, big pressure, early.

'Sometimes I would look up and see the whole table, I mean the whole table, twelve feet by six feet, completely covered with pound notes. All that money, betting on whether or not I was going to win the game, and often just on whether I was going to make a single shot.'

One day, an unemployed Cessnock miner came to Swansea—a fellow known only as 'Dollars Joe'. Eddie was at school at the time, and in his absence Dollars wiped the floor. Took on all comers, beat them, and pocketed the proceeds.

In the end there was only one thing to be done—send for Eddie.

News of the game spread and by the time Eddie arrived the room was filled to bursting with miners and fishermen, all keen to back the local lad. Drinking, smoking, yelling out for Eddie to send Dollars Joe back whence he came, with an empty wallet.

It was somewhere in the middle of that game—Mr Charlton can't remember precisely now—that Eddie felt it. That tell-tale bit of moisture between his legs which meant . . . which meant . . .

'Just excuse me a moment, I'll be back in a sec,' he said, before racing to the bathroom.

'It sometimes happened like that,' Charlton laughed wryly as he told me, 'that the pressure would become so great, that I'd look down and see a wet spot and . . .

And that was that. But back to the business at hand.

At the end of half an hour, to and fro, only the black ball remained, with the game in the balance. Dollars Joe to shoot. The Cessnock man struck hard, hit, but . . . as the pool hall breathed again . . . the black ball wobbled around the pocket and then came out again.

Eddie to play, a straight shot, white ball off the cushion on to the black and hopefully straight into the pocket.

He missed. Eddie missed. Dollars Joe sank the black and won the game.

That night, Eddie was helping his grandfather clean up after everyone had gone—just as he always did—when the old man mentioned that he was going to change the tip on Eddie's cue, that he was sure that that was what had gone wrong.

It was exactly the catalyst Eddie needed to say what was on his mind. 'I'm not bothered, Pop, I'm not going to be using it anymore,' Eddie got out.

'Why?'

'Because I could have beaten him, I really should have beaten him, I'm a better player than he is. But I didn't beat him because I was too nervous, I'm always too nervous, I don't want to do it anymore.'

'That's no reason to give up Eddie. As you get older, you'll get used to it and nerves won't worry you so much.'

'No. I've decided. I'm so upset and disappointed Pop I feel sick, I'm not going to play anymore.'

And they left it at that.

As a matter of fact Eddie held out for as long as two weeks before he picked up a cue again—just to remind himself of what it felt like, mind—and then he started practising again, in spite of himself.

Then, not long after that, Eddie was practising after school, and was half-listening to ol' Joe explain to an old fisherman friend the 'little problem' Eddie had been having with his nerves, when the friend replied with something that stayed with him ever after.

'Well Joe,' said the old man, 'Eddie's opponents ... they're bloody nervous too.'

To Eddie, standing stock-still as he turned the sentence over and over in his mind, it was like a revelation. 'That's right,' I thought. 'They're going to be just as nervous as me, it's just part of the game. What I've got to do is play well *despite* my nerves.'

So Eddie settled down to playing again and ... went on to rule the world!

That fella looks a bit lightweight.
Ahh... but he's heavily tattooed.

# Gong busters

When I was eleven years old, I was advised by a friend to wear purple shorts to rugby trials, as that way the selectors would definitely notice you. A bit over a decade later, the Wallabies halfback Phil Cox confided that the best way to get points in the Rothmans Medal best-and-fairest competition—apart from playing brilliantly—was to go up to the referee at the end of the game, look him right in the eye, and say, 'Good game, Sir.' (Ten minutes later, when he was filling in the form, he would remember you fondly.)

In more recent times, I have heard the theory that markedly blond players tend to win Brownlow Medals, Dally Ms and the like, as they are that much more noticeable.

Laurie Ebert, who describes himself as a 71-year-old GRUMP (GRown Up Mature Person), offers a modern theory: 'In the 'modern game', you have to have as many tattoos covering as much of your body as possible to catch the umpires' eyes—the more hideous the better.' His evidence? The career of Dane Swan.

# The mysteries of modern cricket

I take joy from a comment by Adam Gilchrist a few years ago, concerning the age-old talking point among cricket boffins on whether or not a pitch would or would not take spin on the fifth day.

Well, Gilchrist, who was still playing at the time, said he never looked at the state of a pitch before the beginning of a game, because neither he nor anybody had the slightest clue about whether it would take spin on the fifth day . . .

Steve Waugh, meantime, acknowledged he never looked at the hands of a wrist spinner to see which way the ball came out, to try to work out whether it's going to be a flipper, googly, Chinaman or up-the-Windsor-Road-from-Baulkham-Hills-and-how's-your mother. He just kept his eyes right on the ball the whole way and belted the bloody thing.

# Tooth about Sam

In December 2011 Australian cricket lost Sam Loxton, at the age of 90. He had been one of the last two Invincibles—members of Bradman's 1948 team, which was the first to never lose a match on their tour of England.

One of my spies was at a function, about eighteen months before he died, when Sam was being interviewed. 'Not that he needed that,' my spy recounted. 'He could talk underwater. During the course of the interview, Sam was excitedly telling a story, and his false teeth took off for a risky single, flying over the top of the close-in fielders. Without missing a beat, Sam caught them on their way out and put them back in his mouth and finished the story. I will never forget the moment. He was 88 and still showed reflexes any current international would die for.'

# Kenny, played strong, done good

'The TV business,' Hunter S. Thompson once famously wrote, 'is uglier than most things. It is normally perceived as some kind of cruel and shallow money trench through the heart of the journalism industry, a long plastic hallway where thieves and pimps run free and good men die like dogs . . .'

Just how Kenny Sutcliffe not only survived but prospered in that world for so many decades on end—being popular with the public and workmates alike—was a matter of some discussion in late 2016 when he announced his retirement.

I thought Channel Nine's Executive Producer of Sport, Tom Malone, got closest when he said: 'He did his homework, knew his stuff, made broadcasting look easy, and always had a kind word and a laugh for his fellow broadcasters and the production crew. He has a great sense of fun and irreverence. He's a great team man, and we'll miss him greatly. Has there ever been a greater twinkle in the eye than Ken's?'

Bingo. Everyone who prospers in TV in the long term is able to play to a coveted long suit, and this was Kenny's—that mischievous twinkle in his eyes. It suggested that this next item was such a cracker that, even though he was the presenter, he is only just holding it together. Wait till you see it!

My favourite memory of Ken was a few years ago, on Nine's National News, when a story was presented concerning golfer Mianne Bagger and how she had started life as a man but, after an operation, was now a woman.

The final shot in the story showed Bagger hitting the ball awry. On handing back to the main newsreader, Mark Ferguson, Ken added deadpan, but the eyes gave him away: 'That's a very nasty slice . . .'

# In the beginning

I am Isabel Letham, and Freshwater is my beach.

You see it now, almost as the very picture of a Sydney summer: gambolling kids and sunbaking bodies in the foreground, with flocks of bathers just beyond, wading in the waves as bodysurfers slalom between, and surfers further out engage in their endless hunt for the best break.

Can I tell you that it was oh so different when I was young? As a matter of fact, when I was born in the last gasp of the 19th Century, bathing was illegal in the daylight hours. Bit by bit that began to change though. First Manly lifted the ban on bathing in 1902, and other beaches quickly followed suit—even if those suits still covered most of your body. By 1915 though, when I was just 16, a new phenomenon hit Australia, and it started right here.

A very charismatic man from Hawaii by the name of Duke Kahanamoku came to Sydney, and gave a demonstration of a great Hawaiian passion called 'surf-shooting' to several hundred Sydneysiders, who gathered on the beach on that wet and windy Sunday afternoon of late January. From the first moment when the Duke had paddled out and then turned, onto the face of a breaking wave before *standing up*, we could barely believe what we were seeing, and the extraordinary skill and grace with which he did everything. And then, the most amazing thing of all. After a few waves, the Duke paddled back to the shore and announced that he wanted someone to go back out there with him. And he picked me!

I don't know, some girls might have said no, but I never considered it. Not only did I love the water, but with my mother being a very energetic political activist, I had always been surrounded by strong women whose mantra was that women could do *anything*. So I went with him. I lay on the front of the board, as he paddled from behind, and then we turned . . .

I will never forget that plunging feeling as we went down the first few waves as, despite my initial courage, I couldn't stop myself from yelling for him to stop! The first couple of times he did, but then, he suddenly kept going and we were going down the wave! Then the Duke's big hand came from behind, and pulled me to my feet. It was like nothing I had ever felt before, and I knew at that moment that I was hooked for life.

People credit me with being the first Australian to ever stand up on a surfboard, and whether or not that is true—as there are other claims—one thing is certain. Something changed in Australia that day. There was some loosening of the soul, where before things had been tight; some soaring of the spirit to the skies, where previously so much had been of the earth. Within days, others were starting to make their own boards out of big planks of wood, and it spread from there . . .

Personally, I could never quite get enough of it and in one way or another did it for much of the rest of my active life. When I died in 1995, the local board-riders paddled out beyond the breakers, formed a circle, and scattered my ashes in those same waters that I had loved so much. This greatly pleased my spirit, and the locals say that my spirit lives on, here at Freshwater Beach.

# A word of Warney

The scene was set at the 1999 cricket World Cup when Australia was playing Scotland at Worcestershire. Oh, go on, say you remember!

Late in the match, Scotland is going after the large Australian total, when your favourite and mine, Shane Warne, finds himself fielding way down in deep long-on, in front of a rowdy group of Scots, with a few Pommy blow-ins, who decided it would be a very good idea to pick on our Shane.

There are three reasons.

He is Shane Warne.

He is tabloid fodder from heaven for the British papers, with every day bringing new revelations about what he gets up to on Saturday nights.

He is more than a tad on the portly side. To quote the late, great, P.G. Wodehouse in *Very Good Jeeves*, he is 'a tubby little chap who looked as if he had been poured into his clothes and had forgotten to say "When!"'

But anyhoo, on this day, Warne is down there fielding the odd ball, and, of course, something of an organised choir of Scotsmen starts to form up behind him. Well practiced, they break up into two sections of the choir, and on the cue of the choir leader dropping his raised arm, the first half sing out in a loud mock whisper:

Shane Warne's Grip
for the Steak & Kidney

Reg

*Who ate all the pies?*
*Who ate all the pies?*
*Who ate all the pies?*

The other section of the choir answer, singing in a crescendo:

*Shane did!*
*Shane DID!!*
*SHANE DID!!!!*

And now altogether sing ... 'YOU FAT BASTARD, YOU FAT BASTARD, YOU ATE ALL THE PIES!

Warne being Warne, of course, simply shows them the finger but there is no doubt he is *distinctly* underwhelmed.

Now, whether or not this was the moment for the genesis of Shane Warne deciding, or at least his mum deciding, he needed to take diet pills, we know not—but we do know that that particular exercise all ended in tears.

And doesn't it always?

# Nothing left

When your team is getting hammered and there's nothing left
    to give,
And there's a feeling in your heart that you'd rather die than live,
You know you must hang in there, find something else inside,
Even though you have exhausted all supplies of guts and pride.
Then a tearaway Goliath goes flying through the ruck,
And his body clears defenders like a bullbar on a truck.
In his wake your fallen comrades form a red and bruised collage,
Made of blood and splattered cartilage, battered victims of the
    charge.
Then behind the try line the heads are bowed again,
As the heartache and the pain cuts through 15 beaten men.
A win is now impossible, you start to think out loud,
And you thank Christ that you've retired and you're sitting in
    the crowd!

Murray Hartin

# LOCAL HEROES

...wollongongongone...

*'Mind you, they reckon the only reason Wayne Gardner went so fast is because he pasted two photos of Wollongong in his rear-view mirrors . . .'*

Billy Birmingham, in response to the news that swimmer Leisel Jones imagined a sand crab was pursuing her down the pool.

*'This has been my dream, like, my whole life.'*

Lexi Thompson became the youngest person to win a LPGA event. She's 16.

*'John Howard could have taken wickets on that pitch.'*

Kerry O'Keeffe, on a contributing factor to Bangladesh's stunning victory over the Australian Test team.

*'A lot less washing for one thing.'*

Darren Lockyer's wife, Loren, when asked what his retirement would mean to her.

*'If I'm going to lie on my back for an hour, I expect to be enjoying myself.'*

So said Irish bowling champion Margaret Johnston, who withdrew from her national team after refusing the sports psychologist's request that she lie on a towel for an hour to meditate.

# The kick

There's this bloke, see, Paul Waterhouse, a producer mate of mine from Channel Seven, who I've worked with over many stories for their *Sunday Night* program. Very quietly spoken, extremely self-effacing, devout. But his own story? I had to eke it out of him, practically to the point of holding him by the ankles out the window of a Boston restaurant, and *insist* he tell me something of himself.

Not a lot to tell, he would say, but in terms of passions, the thing that stood out after his love for his wife, Beth, and his love of making television, was Aussie Rules. Growing up in Menangle just outside of Campbelltown, he and his father and three brothers had kicked footballs to each other until their noses bled, and he'd actually been good enough to make the under-15 rep teams for Sydney, playing alongside the likes of Nick Davis, Lenny Hayes and Mark McVeigh, all of whom went on to play AFL. And yes, Paul had dreamed, too, of playing in the big leagues but, by the age of 19 or so, the realisation struck he just wasn't quite good enough: he would never know what it was like to be in a packed stadium, to kick the winning goal, hear the roar of the crowd, and all the rest.

Never mind. Paul got on with it. He joined Channel Seven, rose through the producing ranks, married Beth, and had a baby daughter, Elsie. Throughout he kept close touch with Aussie Rules, following first the Swans and then the Giants. Life was good, and if Paul sometimes wondered, idly, what it would have been like to have kicked the winning goal himself, it was no more than a passing thought as he waited for the traffic lights to change, rather than any solid regret.

Still, there he was with Beth and their daughter one Saturday, attending a Giants v Swans game when, at quarter-time, one of the Swans fans taps them on the shoulder and says, 'Hey isn't that you guys up on the screen?'

It is! And the ground announcer is saying Paul has been selected at random to have a go at three-quarters time at winning $100,000 by attempting to kick a football into a pile of Toyo tyres, 30 metres away. If it goes in, he gets $100K!

Paul is stunned.

And so is Beth. She imagines him kicking the ball in and them celebrating. And what it would mean for their mortgage, for Elsie's future . . . But she pushes such thoughts away, and comes back to reality. Of course that won't happen. Still, she can't help herself and does lean over to Paul, to say, 'Babe, if anyone can do it, you can. But no pressure. Don't think about it too much.'

Paul can't think of anything else! Excusing himself from Beth, he heads down to the concourse at the back of the stands, where an eight-year-old kid has a footy. For the next hour or so, Paul and the kid kick back and forth, as the old rhythms start to come back, his hand-eye-foot co-ordination, the way to kick the ball, so it soars, just like his father had taught him all those years ago. He tries to visualise what it will be like, the task that awaits, just how to kick it and . . .

And it is time. His name is being called out. Beth and little Elsie come down to give him a kiss and wish him luck. 'No pressure,' Beth says one more time, giving him a hug. 'Just block out the crowd and give it a go. I think you can get it in.'

And suddenly, he is living the dream: out there, under the lights, on the wide turf, with the ball in hand, as the crowd roars!

Well, sort of. It is more a happy rumble than anything. The Giants are ahead and have every chance of pulling off an astounding win over the Swans, and this goal-kicking comp is a bit of fun that happens every Giants home game. Of course no one has ever kicked it, but still. Let's watch him on the big screen.

'Mate,' the sound-man says to Paul as he lines it up, 'I've seen a few of these. Now, whatever you do, make sure you go high. Go straight, and just try and get your depth right, which is the tricky thing.'

Good point. Paul steadies himself. Lines it up. Blocks out the noise of the crowd, just as Beth had suggested. All he can hear now is the ground announcer giving the count-down: '5, 4, 3, 2, 1 . . .'

Paul trots forward. Kicks . . .

It connects well. The ball soars high, and it looks pretty good from the get-go. Wobbles to the left a little, but he's made allowance for the breeze and it's straightening. It's heading roughly towards the pile of tyres and . . .

Standing to the side with the PR people, Beth can hardly bear to watch, but makes herself. It is like, seriously, time is standing still as the ball comes down and . . .

And hits the back of the stack, right on the inside lip!

It wobbles, bounces, thinks about bouncing out again, but . . . SUDDENLY-GOES-IN!

Paul comes to.

The crowd is going completely NUTS! He's *kicked* it! He's KICKED it! It is like every childhood dream come true, only better, as not even players get to kiss the love of their lives straight after they score the winning goal! For now, after charging around

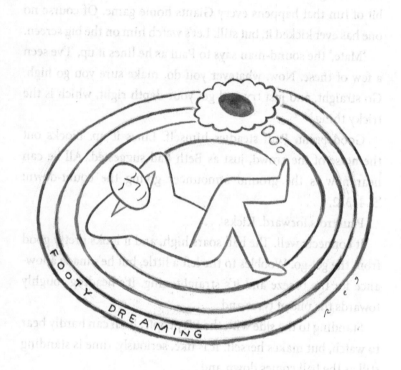

FOOTY DREAMING

like a mad thing, fists in the air, suddenly, here is Beth, roaring over and over to their daughter, 'Daddy kicked the football! Daddy kicked the football!' And now the Giants themselves, running back to their positions for the fourth quarter, are yelling their congrats. Leaving the field at last, Paul picks up baby Elsie as if she is a trophy and holds *her* up to the crowd.

They roar back.

On the trip home Paul calls his father and all three of his brothers. Under the lights, he'd kicked the ball on target, to the roar of the crowd. At the age of 36, he'd lived the dream.

# Bravo the surf dancer

A yonk ago, I ran a yarn about a young girl, Pacha Light, who danced in front of a sign saying 'BUSKING FOR A BOARD' at the Roxy Pro surfing event on the Gold Coast, the day before her tenth birthday.

So there she was, dancing up a storm to the music coming from the portable CD player she had brought along for the occasion, while her proud mother watched on. People stopped, watched and started putting some coins in the old grey felt hat she had by the sign. The sun shone, the people smiled, and Pacha danced.

And then along came the 18-year-old North Narrabeen pro surfer, Laura Enever, who not only stopped, but started dancing with her. All the people smiled some more, and then the pro surfer suddenly disappeared. She returned a short time later with one of her back up surfboards, which she gave to the young girl. Using an indelible marker, she wrote these words on the board:

*To Dear Pacha,*
*You're the most amazing dancer EVER.*
*Now have some fun in the surf'.*
*Laura Enever.*

After getting this board, Pacha practised every day after school, through the summer and into the winter. As the years

reg

clicked over, she got stronger and stronger. Then one day her mother wrote to advise me that Pacha has been picked in the Australian junior surfing team going to Portugal!

Bravo, Pacha, and well done to Laura Enever.

# The derro with the kero

When the Olympic torch first visited our shores, in the lead-up to the 1956 Olympic Games, Sydney was agog with excitement when it arrived in our city on its journey south. Tens of thousands of Sydneysiders lined the streets all those years ago, with the thickest knot being around Sydney Town Hall, where the then lord mayor, Pat Hills, was due to receive it from cross-country champion Harry Dillon and make a speech—*the Olympic spirit, faster, higher, stronger, Sydney delighted, etc., etc.*—before passing it on to another runner, Bert Button.

Waiting. Waiting. Waiting. There! A massive roar from the crowd goes up as the runner with a flame comes into view, and the police escort presses tight to keep him safe. He bounds up the stairs and hands the torch to the lord mayor, who begins to launch into . . .

But then someone whispers into his ear and he realises something is amiss. What is he holding? Nothing less than a chair leg, to which is attached a pair of kerosene-soaked underpants. (Cue Bill Lawrie: *'Got him, yes! It's all happening here at Sydney Town Hall! That is the greatest get, you will ever see!'*)

In fact, the real Olympic runner was still blocks away, and this hoax runner, Barry Larkin, was a Sydney Uni student from St John's College. He was making a protest, drawing everyone's

attention to the fact that it had been the Nazis who'd started the whole torch relay concept.

Upon his return to the uni, Larkin received a standing ovation from his fellow students.

# Sign of the times

It is 1 pm on a Saturday in May, up at the Koola ovals at Killara. On one field there is a classic suburban rugby game with the local lads giving some equally rough 'n' ready 'n' rotund visitors a pretty solid work-over.

On the next field is a UTS women's soccer game.

Then comes the rain and the wind. Who knows what kind of storm is about to blow up? Just to be sure, the rugby lads run for shelter.

The women play on, one of them receiving a yellow card for unnecessary roughness.

# Top of the pops

In May seven-year-old Darby played his first game of rugby league for the Clovelly Crocodiles. After the game, just as has happened for many generations, he and the other newcomers to the team were presented with a club medallion by their coach, now 82-years-old, affectionately known to all as Pops. On the back of it is engraved:

*Darby Murphy*
*Good Luck for the future.*
*AIM HIGH.*
*Always do your best.*
*Never ever give up.*
*Study, Train and Play hard.*
*Be a loyal team member.*
*Be a good winner & gracious loser.*
*Above all look after your mind and body.*
*Pops.*

Good on ya, Pops.

# How Kurt scored the try of a lifetime

Forget the rugby, the cricket, the drugs in sport, the suspensions and all the rest for a bit, OK? Think instead on Kurt Longford. A good man, a 27-year-old who lives in Narrandera with his single mother. Kurt is autistic, on a disability pension, and has not necessarily always found it easy to fit in. Generally, however, sport has been the exception and this year, after a long time with the Bidgee Hurricanes, he joined Wagga's rugby league club Brothers, slotting into their reserve grade side and usually coming on from the reserves bench near the end.

No, he's not a world-beater, but he's dead keen, plays his heart out, never misses a training session or a game, and his fine mother, Pauline, is thrilled at Kurt being with them, as she knows that both the Brothers players, and even the opposition, look after him.

And he doesn't mind a chat, our Kurt. He can remember everything about every game he's ever played—who was in his team, and the other, and exactly what happened. And to his dying day, he'll remember what happened last Sunday ...

See, late in the game, the Brothers bolter, Buddy O'Neill, bursts through one opponent and dodges another before the men from Junee—Laurie Daley country, after all—close in on him like mad things and hit him hard. Still, somehow, Buddy gets away the miracle pass to ... someone who is looming on his left, and charging like a runaway steam train.

It is KURT LONGFORD!

Kurt hauls the ball in, steps left, steps right and, despite the defence again closing hard, smashes over the line and gets the ball down.

Try! Try! TRY!

A TRY FOR YOUR LIFE!

The Brothers boys go crazy in congratulations, as do the Junee Diesels. In fact, all 25 men on the field crowd round to shake his hand, give him a hug and a pat on the back. Kurt walks back for the kick-off, suddenly the tallest man on the field, as in the stands it is not just his mother who is weeping. For the whole grandstand is rising in acclaim, as he salutes them in turn.

At the end of the match, won by Brothers, Kurt leads the team victory song in the dressing rooms and then it takes him no less than an hour to get to the car park, as everyone at the ground wants to talk about his try, and he wants to talk to them. At length!

That evening, at Wagga's Vic Hotel, the Brothers and Junee players gather around, roaring out *I Love to have a Drink with Kurt*, while his mother waits in the car outside to get him safely back to Narrandera.

# Tri-er honoured

Imagine the scene. While the rest of Sydney sat in gridlocked
traffic on Sunday morning, 1500 triathletes were running,
riding and swimming from first light. Of course, once one has
finished such an event, the general thing is to burst through
the finish line before collapsing to the ground as you allow the
blessed feeling of achievement to wash over you. Then the form
is to stagger back to the 'transition zone' to retrieve your bike.
But there is a strict protocol involved. It is considered very poor
form to get that bike until the last competitor has completed
the cycle course.

So it was that on Sunday morning, a hundred or so of the
first finishers, all of them as lean as greyhounds, wander over
to find that, although it is more than two hours since they had
gone through this section, they still can't get on their bikes and
go home, because there are still competitors who haven't gone
through yet. So they wait, some more patiently than others.

Finally though, a good ten minutes after the penultimate
competitor, the last man arrives. He's hurting, but he's still going.
A large bull of a man of oriental appearance, he either dismounts
or falls off his carbon-fibre steed—it's hard to tell—and jogs very,
very slowly, with his bike towards the transition.

Many hundreds of eyes watch on in a curious silence until
suddenly, in a beautiful moment, the swollen crowd rises in
unison to clap and cheer with genuine warmth, encouragement

and appreciation for the efforts of a fellow competitor who is struggling, but still game.

The big man remains a study of exhausted, single-minded focus, but now continues with a slight spring in his step. Gotta love this city.

# Bringing people together

Amelia Derrett is a 14-year-old schoolgirl who plays in a girls cricket side up Thornleigh way. She is not just any player—she is partially blind with ocular albinism, and has tried to make the grade over the summer by bowling tennis balls in the backyard with a family dog, who has played 'fetch' until his little legs can fetch no more.

Just how blind is Amelia? Blind enough that, last week when she was bowling, she heard what sounded like the stumps rattling a couple of seconds after the ball left her hands. It was only when her teammates engulfed her—cheering, slapping her on the back—that she was able to confirm it.

'I was very excited because before that I sucked like every person does in their first few games,' she said. 'I honestly thought my disability would hold me back from everything. I was always scared it would hold me back in life . . . I love team sports because I get to play with people.'

# The beauty of Brock

Following the death of beloved rugby figure David Brockhoff, I received many lovely reminiscences from readers about their dealings with him. Mark Kenna from Sydney's Scots College reported that, for much of the past three decades, it was almost a rite of passage for the coaches and players of the First XV to have a 'session with Brock'. Towel around his neck, tucked into his track-suit, he would unleash in classic fashion, holding the ball up for all to see, and with help from my friends, this is what he was like:

'It's in the noodle fellas. Passed down from God himself through Moses, Danie Craven, then to Brock. The fruit boys, the FRUIT! You'll run out, you'll line up on the other side of halfway, and . . . no excuses, cause havoc at the breakdown like sharks in a school of mullet. And when you're through the other side we're like crowbars through the Opera House window. We get in, loot the joint and get out. Quick feed to the Dancing Man all day fellas, all day like wind through the wheat. Centre stage, I want to see arms through the briar bushes and dinosaur steps through the guts. And boys, when we get to the top of the mountain, grand piano stuff—we plant the flag! Above all, slaughter house, Friday night fight night at the old showgrounds, blood on the floor. We must have the fruit, so every lineout a dockyard brawl. But not in our 22. There, row of ministers.'

Coaches learnt to bring him in on a Tuesday, because it often took the rest of the week to explain to the players what he had said. But the Scots teams always lifted on the weekend after their time with Brock.

The day after his death, it was interesting to note that Scots, wearing black armbands, were victorious in all four senior grades against rivals St Joseph's College at Hunters Hill, a result the school had not achieved in living memory. Brock would have been very proud indeed.

# Barrackers to the fore

A contribution from Sydneysider Matt Cleary: 'One morning, a couple of weeks ago, as I was jogging along New South Head Road in Double Bay, I idly thought that with the cricket season approaching . . . I'd break up the pounding rhythm of the run by practising my bowling run-up, delivery stride and rolling of the arm thereover.

'Just as I was through my third delivery a bloke leaned from the passenger seat of a speeding removals van and yelled, "Howizzeeeee!?!", as blokes leaning from [said vehicles] are wont to do.

'Last Thursday lunchtime, I was jogging again, this time along the Harbour Bridge heading towards North Sydney for a swim and again I was into bowling practice. Just as I was through what might've been a pretty good fast-medium offering, a guy yelled from the passenger seat of another van, "No ball!!!" and I gave pause to reflect: what a great country we live in.

'Soon after, though, the peach: as I approached the steps which lead down to Kirribilli, an old digger, a man who'd seen better days, who'd obviously been studying my imaginary thunderbolts, looked me up and down, and said, "Who the f@&# are you? F@&#in' Warney?"'

# Marc making his

This is the story of Marc Reichler-Stillhard, a fine young fellow, born with Down's syndrome up Yamba way, and immediately embraced by the local community of the mighty Clarence Valley, where the river flows fast, the fields grow green and the local folk are strong. Integrated with mainstream classes at the local schools and signed up with local sporting clubs, Marc has been a beloved figure, who has learnt as much from the kids around him, as they have learnt from him.

On a sunny day in March 2015, see, the young lads of Yamba are playing the game of their lives against the boys of nearby Lawrence in the local under-12 cricket grand final. No quarter asked for or given, Lawrence has set a good total, but the Yamba young'uns are a confident breed and they go out hard after it. And they get there, too.

The scores are level with two balls to go! Yamba's last man on strike is Marc and, as he walks to the crease, the crowd holds its breath.

What is going to happen?

The second last ball is bowled, Marc swings valiantly and . . . misses. One ball to go. The Lawrence bowler—a good sport with a fine instinct that some things are more important than mere trophies, a credit to his town—sends down an easier ball. This time young Marc connects, and starts to run like a scalded hare, but the ball is in the air. The Lawrence fieldsman runs in to take the catch . . . but drops it.

Yamba wins. Marc is carried off the field on the shoulders of *both* teams, as the crowd roars.

What's not to like? What's not to weep about?

# Irish pluck

The Swans' great Irishman, Tadgh Kennelly, was invited to give the speech at the AFL grand final dinner—in the presence of the prime minister—and it was reportedly the best in years. Here is a quick burst:

'As my career began to take off in the beautiful surroundings of Sydney, there were still a lot of challenges I had to overcome. Yes, I was in a country that spoke the same language as myself but have you guys ever sat back and listened to the Australian lingo? Especially inside a football club, it's like being in the middle of Russia. I had no idea what was being said to me half the time, so much so that during a game in my early days the then senior coach, Rodney Eade, ran out at quarter-time and came straight up to me screaming: "Just bomb it long down the guts." I must have had a look of utter bemusement as I had absolutely no idea what he meant, and went straight up to our assistant coach to find out my instructions.

'I remember one pre-season training session when I had just arrived back from Ireland after my Christmas break where the weather was, well, let's just say mild. We were doing a 10-kilometre run and let's just say the weather in Sydney was a wee bit warmer than a mild Irish Christmas. I started to feel light-headed and, before I knew it, I had passed out and I was in the back of an ambulance.

'I started to come around and our captain at the time, Paul Kelly, was with me in the back of the ambulance. One of the paramedics asked me my name, and I said, "Tadhg", and he said, "Spell it", so I did. And as I spelt it out, he looked at Kell and said, "This kid is off his head, get him to hospital quick—what kind of name is that?!"'

# Goaaaaaaal

You have to imagine the scene. The mighty Budgewoi Bulldogs under-15 rugby league side were lined up against their Ourimbah Magpies counterparts, only to find the Maggies so big and so strong that, with seconds remaining, the Budgie boys were on the wrong side of a 56-0 thrashing. (And really, at this stage, they had been lucky to get to nil.)

But what the hell? Determined to trouble the scorer at least once on their account, when the ball comes to the Bulldogs' halfback just as the ref is about to blow full-time, the lad, young Ben Selmes, decides to make a point. From 35 metres out, near the sideline, he decides to have a go at a field-goal, and nails the kick of his life.

From somewhere in the heavens, Frank Hyde himself could have called it: 'It's long, it's high, it's STRAIGHT BETWEEN THE POSTS!' Appreciative supporters from both clubs simply stand and applaud the plucky kid for breaking the Bulldogs' duck in such impressive style. Hooter sounds, and the final score is 56-1.

And what will you have, son? Another round? Well, here you go.

In round 14, the two teams met again, and it was like déjà vu all over again. Again, Budgewoi are again getting hammered, and again they're desperate. Why, this looks like a job for Super Ben. And there he is! The ball comes to him, even as the

Ourimbah lads—haven't they seen this movie before?—rush him. He steadies, shapes . . . and unleashes! The final score: 56-1.

Ain't sport grand? And good on you, Ben. On the receiving end of a belting like that, the firm rule is: if you can't beat them, take a piece of them home with you to show your mother or, at the very least, make sure the scoreboard ticks over at least once.

Both times, Budgewoi had a point to make, and they made it!

# Going the tonk

The great Sachin Tendulkar visited Bradman Oval at Bowral on Thursday morning, where, among other things, he offered some advice to a group of schoolboys on how to be a successful batsman.

'Let your subconscious mind respond,' he said, with the gravity of one who has a century of centuries for India to his credit.

But schoolboy Alex Biggs was having none of it: 'My subconscious mind says "just tonk it", but that does not work all the time.'

Laughter all round.

# Share the love

The Avoca Sharks took on the Gosford Red Devils in the local grand final. Gosford was far too strong for the Sharks, running out winners 26-10. After the game, both teams trotted off to their respective clubhouses—one to celebrate a magnificent win, the other to celebrate a magnificent decade. As the night unfolded, the Sharks made their way to the Central Coast Hotel and the two teams came face to face.

As reader Josh Davies told me: 'Here's where the "Why I love rugby" part comes in. For rather than a stare-down/stand-off/don't-look-at-me sideways atmosphere, players from both clubs embraced. Congratulations and commiserations were passed, shouts were started, high fives, man-cuddles and head rubs filled the air. Both teams partied on into the wee hours truly together, there was never a harsh word spoken, nor the risk of any disagreement or donnybrook erupting.

'An outsider would have had no idea this was two opposing teams, that only hours earlier had been driving each other into the turf—to an outsider, this would have appeared to be ONE team celebrating. Like I said—I don't know that there's many other codes of sport that could pull that off.' I agree.

# All the marbles

A nice kind of bloke is Kingswood sewing machine repairman Terry Rastall, even if he has lost his marbles. But already I am ahead of myself . . .

See, just three weeks ago, Terry had a call from a woman from Haberfield wanting her machine repaired, giving an address that he immediately recognised as the childhood home he and his family had moved from forty years earlier. As he entered the premises, the years fell away. Those long hot summers! The other neighbourhood kids! The fun in the backyard! Ah, yes, the backyard. Back then, Terry had been *the* hotshot marble player in the neighbourhood and so loved the game, and was so good, that he had collected close on 500 marbles, his prize possession. Some said he was the best in the whole suburb, maybe the whole *city*. And now, in conversation with the woman of the house, Terry admits his principal regret in leaving this old place was the fact that on the day of departure, his naughty brother had grabbed all these marbles and spread them all over the backyard!

Funny he should say that. For the nice lady brightens up and says that for the past forty years, while toiling in the garden, hanging out the washing and all the rest, she has been finding, cleaning and collecting those marbles and . . . keeping them in a container in the laundry! Would Terry like them back? He would! Excitedly, Terry takes the precious container home, and counts them up—342 of the beauties!

But the story gets better still. For when he tells his mates the story, those mates tell him about the Australian Marbles Championships coming up in Brunswick Heads. Terry decides to take on the challenge with his old marbles, starts practising, then travels up for the tournament. And all the old skills come back.

Winning round after round, he makes it all the way to the three-game final and then takes the title from four-time winner Andrew Hanlon, two games to one. He is now, officially, the best marbles player in all of *Australia*.

# Now, now, Nowra

The mighty Nowra Warriors rugby league team, despite a formidable pedigree, had a tough year back in 2003, failing to win a match and frequently giving the scoreboard attendants RSI as opposing teams ran up 60-and-70-point drubbings. In July, though, all the planets were misaligned to deliver a new agony on a stormy afternoon as they took on the highly ranked Albion Park side.

And it really was stormy. So stormy that after the game, Warriors captain-coach Adrian Weller was quoted in Nowra's newspaper, the *South Coast Register,* thus: 'You know you're having a bad day when, at 98-4 down, you're huddled behind the line waiting for a conversion kick and lightning strikes the post next to you . . .'

Reg

# Top-class effort

They had the Balmain Fun Run last Sunday, as ever in the grounds of Rozelle's Callan Park, with a mixture of families, fun-runners, kids, and serious athletes who ran like scalded cats. The distances varied from 2 kilometre, to 5 kilometre, to 10 kilometre. At the conclusion, when all the races have been run and won, the organisers are midway through giving prizes and trophies to some of Australia's best athletes, when the MC gets a tap on the back and is told, 'Check it out, there's one last kid coming down the straight.'

And there is. A young lad with cerebral palsy—with crutches, and an adult assisting on each side—bravely doing his best to finish the 2 kilometre race he started well over half an hour before.

To his credit, the MC stops the presentation cold and says, 'While it's wonderful to recognise the best, it's important to make sure we honour effort as well, and there has been no bigger effort than the young lad coming down the straight—get on over and give him a cheer.'

With which, every spectator, every sponsor, every stall holder rushes to the fence and a huge roar erupts, building from the last 50 metres onwards, and EXPLODING as the six-year-old breasts the tape.

Not a dry eye in the house.

Well done, Arran Keith. You are a champion.

# My favourite yarn of the lot

In March 2004, one of my spies reported being in Newcastle to see the Roosters vs Knights game, when he noticed in the half-time mini-game between a couple of under-8 teams that one of the young players had physical disabilities, probably cerebral palsy. No matter, he was clearly running around having the time of his life. Even more significant was the way the members of his own side and that of the opposition treated this courageous little bloke. In just about every set of six, his team's first instinct was to look for him first, and see if they could give him the ball to have a run.

The opposition, obviously aware that he couldn't genuinely compete on an even playing field and in the true spirit of what junior sport should be about, of course tackled him, but in a manner that was certain not to inflict any harm on this young hero. On one occasion, he even managed to off-load a ball to a teammate who picked the ball up and scored a try. The crowd loved it and he received warm applause from both his own team and that of the opposition.

His name, as it turned out, is Harry Rodgers—referred to as 'H' by his teammates—and by the following year he was playing for the mighty Kotara Bears junior side in the under-9s. I was advised by his coach that Harry has a condition known as amyoplasia, which affects the joints and muscles. In Harry's case it means he wears splints on his legs and he has had to adapt as best he can with minimal use of his hands. When playing football, Harry catches and passes with his elbows. The cooperation of other teams has been fantastic. They allow the coach to go onto the field when Harry is playing, because when he has been tackled he needs some help getting to his feet.

It turned out that one of the avowed ambitions of his team-mates this year, beyond winning the best they can, was to get Harry over the try line or bust. Alas, with 30 seconds to go in the final game of the season, against a strong Wests team, that ambition had remained unfulfilled. And yet . . .

And yet, now the ball comes to our Harry, on the left side of the field, about 30 metres out. There is still a chance! With all his teammates forming a kind of protective cocoon around him, the whole team charges for the line with Harry the hero in the middle. The young lads of Wests—playing with exactly the right spirit and aware of the significance of the moment—do their more or less best to break through the cocoon, but one way or another Harry manages to crashes through for a—try, *try*, TRY!—a try for your life, I'll tell a man it is! Instantly, he is awash in the exhilaration of *both* teams.

And still Harry isn't done. As the final bell sounds, it is Harry who, having practised his kicking all week, lines up the conversion and slots the . . . GOAAAL!

He is carried from the field on the shoulders of his teammates, and taken to the cheering crowd, where a lovely woman weeping tears of triumph engulfs him in joyous embrace.

# The Great War

*Dear Dad,*

*Remember the day that you took me to town and we went to the SCG?*

*You bought me a flag and we stood on the Hill and I sat on your shoulders to see.*

*And remember my words when the game reached its end, How I said what I wanted to do?*

*I said, 'That was great, Dad, and when I grow up, I'll play for Australia, too'.*

*Well, here I am, Dad, I've stayed true to my word but it's not how I hoped it would be.*

*The crowds have all gone and the ground is a mess and there's nobody cheering for me.*

*I'm hungry and cold but I'm starting to sweat, mere words can't describe how I feel.*

*I'm not in a jersey, I'm not wearing shorts and my first cap is made out of steel.*

*My gut's in a knot and I almost feel sick, I've gone two whole days without sleep.*

*My feet are quite damp for we walked most the night through mud that was six inches deep.*

*I'm nervous as hell and I can't settle down, I keep wondering how well I'll do.*

*But I guess that's just normal and how it should be on the
eve of my national debut.*

*The waiting's the worst thing, we just sit around.*

*What happens is out of our hands.*

*We all feel like pawns in a big game of chess,*

*Swapping lives for a small stretch of land.*

*So many have fallen, it seems such a waste.*

*To say this is fun is a lie.*

*I'll do what I'm told and I'll keep my head down,*

*And I'll pray that the Lord's on my side.*

*Well, Dad, I must go for we're ready to start, it seems we've
been given the word.*

*The silence is eerie, the boys are all quiet, our heartbeat's the
only sound heard.*

*We'll stick with each other, we'll fight till we drop, we'll each
give far more than our best.*

*Tell Mum I am happy, I ask for no more, for this is the
ultimate test.*

*Your son.*

This was written by my mate, Mick Colliss, a keen rugby
player who wanted to be a Wallaby, but rose no higher than
Eastwood Seconds. No matter. If he couldn't represent Australia
in rugby, what about something else? Realising there was no team
representing Australia at the World Sudoku Championships, he
formed a team of mates, who bought themselves some green
blazers with the Australian crest, attended and got thumped.
Mick wrote a book about it, and now makes a fortune on the
speaking circuit!